This book is a gift
to the

Carbondale Public Library

from

The Roaring Fork Quilt Guild

December 2022

"More desirable than gold... and sweeter than honey..."

That's what Psalm 19 says about Bible truths—
the same rich truths presented just for kids
in Questar's **Gold'n'Honey Books**

QUESTAR PUBLISHERS, INC.
SISTERS, OREGON

The Bible
Tells Me So

The BEGINNER'S GUIDE to
Loving & Understanding
God's Word

MACK THOMAS
Illustrated by JERRY WERNER

CONTENTS

A Note to Parents & Teachers

In *The Bible Tells Me So* we want to help children gain a love for the Scriptures as they see the big picture of what the Bible is all about—its exalted themes, its divine nature and careful structure, and its life-giving power.

The heart of this book includes eight major sections that present these foundations for biblical understanding:

- **the Bible's major divisions;**
- **the Bible's major themes, especially as they relate to God's holy and loving character;**
- **the inspiring story of how God preserved the Bible for us down through the ages;**
- **the Bible as our spiritual food;**
- **the Bible as our guide to everyday living;**
- **the centrality of Christ in all of Scripture;**
- **the Bible's place in the church.**
- and finally, **the geographical and cultural environment in which the Bible was written;**

Along the way, we want to convey with conviction and clarity the Bible's inspiration, the Bible's inerrancy, and the Bible's authority.

All this is great to know for every Christian, but many of us haven't learned as much about the Bible as we would like. Perhaps one reason is that our imaginations aren't always captured by the *excitement* of it all.

So, to build enjoyment and appreciation in our children, in this book we present Bible knowledge in a setting of childhood joys and adventures—from helicopter rides and tree climbs to a backyard show and playground action. These form a backdrop for learning about the deep and lasting satisfaction to be found in the Book of Books.

Our prayer is that this book will help all our sons and daughters to grow in the commitment expressed in one of their happiest songs:

The B—I—B—L—E—
yes, that's the book for me!
I stand alone on the Word of God—
the B-I-B-L-E!

On page **446** in the back of the book you'll find a week-by-week guide for using *The Bible Tells Me So* in a class setting.

The author gratefully acknowledges the worthy assistance
of these works in preparing *The Bible Tells Me So:*

Christian Theology by Millard J. Erickson (Baker Book House, 1983)

The Life Application Bible, New International Version (Tyndale House Publishers, Inc., and Zondervan Publishing House, 1991)

The NIV Study Bible (Zondervan Publishing House, 1985)

Boyd's Bible Handbook by Robert T. Boyd (Harvest House Publishers, 1983)

Halley's Bible Handbook by Henry H. Halley (Zondervan Publishing House, 1927-1965)

Unger's Bible Handbook by Merrill F. Unger (Moody Press, 1966)

Eerdmans' Handbook to the Bible, edited by David Alexander and Pat Alexander (William B. Eerdmans Publishing Company, 1973)

The Illustrated Bible Dictionary (InterVarsity Press and Tyndale House Publishers, 1962, 1980)

Manners and Customs of Bible Lands by Fred H. Wright (Moody Bible Institute, 1953)

Machines, Buildings, Weaponry of Biblical Times by Max Schwartz (Fleming H. Revell, 1990)

The Expositors Bible Commentary, Frank E. Gaebelein, general editor (Zondervan Publishing House, 1979-1991)

Your Bible: From Its Beginning until Now by Edward W. Goodrick (1982)

The Chicago Statement on Biblical Inerrancy (International Council on Biblical Inerrancy, 1978)

Exposition and notes on Psalm 119 in *The Treasury of David* by Charles Haddon Spurgeon

Everyday Life in Bible Times (National Geographic Society, 1967)

with special appreciation to V. Gilbert Beers, for his inspiring example of leading children to a love of God's Word

The Bible Tells Me So

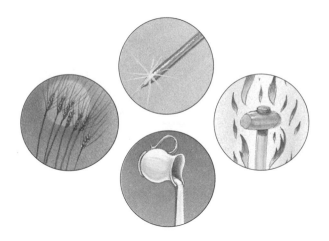

JESUS loves me!

This I know—

for the Bible tells me so…

On the Edge of Discovery

*Why the Bible Is So Different
from All Other Books*

1 With Skyler Brown on the smooth, lazy river that afternoon were four children…each one learning something new about dragonflies.

All around the two canoes, the flying dragons darted and dashed. Often they would hover in the same place like a helicopter. That gave the children a better look at their slender bodies and shiny wings. Then suddenly they would shoot away, as if they had just turned on a jet engine.

"They're so fast!" exclaimed Nancie, who was sharing a canoe with Ian. (Jackson and Krista were with Skyler in the other one.)

"The fastest of all insects," Skyler called out from the other canoe. "I've read that they can fly at speeds of up to forty miles an hour. And they can burst away in any direction: up, down, or to the side. But they're not in danger of running into anything. With their big, bulging eyes they can see in all directions at once."

"What a blast!" said Jackson.

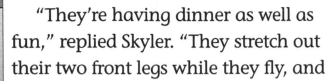

"They're having dinner as well as fun," replied Skyler. "They stretch out their two front legs while they fly, and scoop other bugs right out of the air. Then they eat them without even taking time to land."

"They sound like dragons, all right," said Krista.

"But such beautiful dragons!" said Nancie. "Captain Skyler, *everything* out here seems so beautiful today. Thank you for bringing us." She lifted her face to feel the sun's warm rays.

"Yeah, *thanks!*" echoed Ian.
He was dipping his gleaming paddle into
the water with another graceful J-stroke.
"I could do this forever!"

"I'm glad you like the river as much as I do," said Skyler. "And I'm especially glad you notice all the beauty out here. I think it's telling us something—don't you?"

"You mean...the *beauty* is telling us something?" said Jackson.

"Yeah!" Skyler answered. "Dragon-flies dancing in the air, and rivers flowing to the sea, and the golden sun shining down on us. All of it *tells us* something—don't you think?"

Everyone was quiet. Jackson and Krista and Nancie and Ian were listening for... for what?

"I don't hear much," Jackson finally said.

"Me either," said Ian. During the long silence, a dragonfly had landed on his head.

"Same here," said Nancie. "But even the quietness is beautiful!"

"Yeah, isn't it?" smiled Skyler. "Even the quietness is sending us a signal. And if you listen with *more* than your ears—if you listen with your mind and your heart as well—you'll get the right message. You'll understand that *God is real*—that He's truly there, and that He's so very *powerful!*"

Skyler stopped paddling a moment, and looked around at them all. "And if all this beauty doesn't make you thankful to God, then you're getting the wrong message.

"Because in Romans 1, the Bible says God can clearly be seen in the things He's created.* Those things, of course, include dragonflies and rivers."

"And the sky and sunshine, too!" Nancie said.

"Yep," Skyler nodded. "In fact, Psalm 19 in the Bible starts out like this: '*The heavens are telling the glory of God, and the skies announce what his hands have made.*'"

* On page 442 you'll find a list of the complete Scripture references for this and other Bible passages mentioned in this book.

"So," Jackson said with a smile,
"the weather forecast for today is:
Lots of telling and lots of announcing!"

Everyone laughed. Then Krista laid her paddle in front of her, resting it across each side of the canoe. "So is that how you find out more about God?" she asked. "You go on canoe trips and hikes and do outdoor things like this?"

"Sure," said Skyler. "That's *part* of how a person finds out about Him—*if* that person really wants to know.

"For we also read in Romans 1 that even though God's hand can be seen in the things He's made, many people refuse to see it. They won't give glory to God, and they won't give Him thanks—even though the truth about God is as plain as the nose on their face—or the dragonfly on their head, as the case may be!"

> **SUPER TRUTH**
> *God tells us clearly about Himself in the things He's created.*

"I think I get the message," Ian said. "It's like this: When God created the world, He built in some great clues to help us be sure that *He's* the One who really made it."

"Ian, I couldn't have put it better myself," Skyler said, as the two canoes rounded a wide bend in the river. Before them was a straight stretch of shallow water between two banks of willow trees. Here and there a splashing fish broke the glassy surface.

And there were lots more dragonflies.

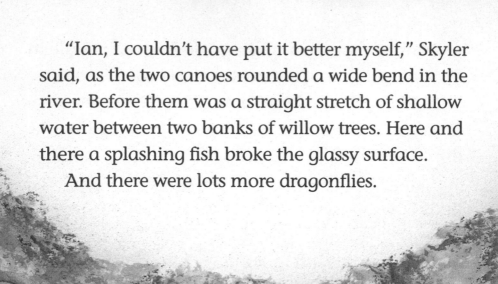

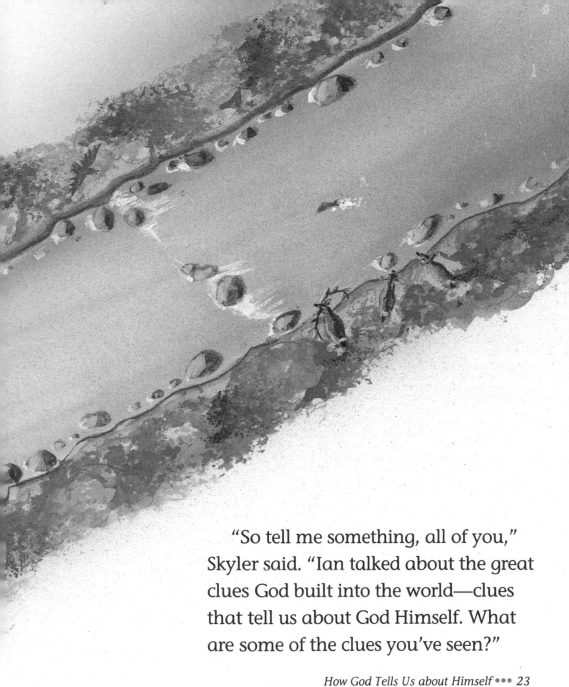

"So tell me something, all of you," Skyler said. "Ian talked about the great clues God built into the world—clues that tell us about God Himself. What are some of the clues you've seen?"

"Sand—and snowflakes!" said Nancie.

"That's right," Jackson said. "Each grain of sand is different from every other grain of sand, and no two snow-flakes are exactly alike either — even though there are zil-lions and zil-lions of them."

"Oh, and here's another one," Krista said: "The planet earth is exactly the right dis-tance from the sun so we don't get cooked and we don't get frozen."

"I know another clue," said Ian. "Water from all the rivers in the world keeps running into the oceans, yet the sea never overflows. Some of the ocean water rises up into clouds, and the clouds blow over the land. Then they drop rainwater, and that water flows back into the rivers."

"It would take Someone amazingly smart and amazingly powerful to put all of that together," Krista said. "It just had to be God!"

"You've got it," Skyler agreed.

Jackson had an extra serious look on his face. "Hey, guys! I've discovered something else amazing: This river water has something special about it— after it comes down from the clouds and flows down here. *It doesn't even feel wet!*"

"Really?" said Ian.

"What do you mean?" Nancie asked.

Jackson's face broke into a grin. "Here, feel for yourself!" he exclaimed, as he swung his paddle into the river and sent a giant splash toward the other canoe.

Nancie and Ian were dripping wet—and laughing at Jackson's joke.

"I guess it's time for a water fight," Skyler said. "And after we're all soaked, I have some more *amazing* things for us to talk about. Right, Jackson?"

With that, Skyler took his paddle and splashed water all over his canoe partner.

The water fight was on!

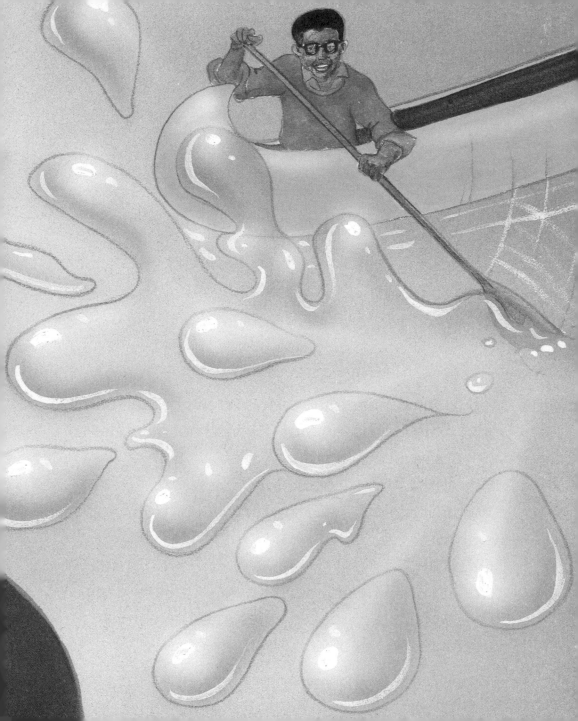

2 Half an hour later, the two crews beached their canoes on a sandbar. They all got out to lie on the sand and dry off.

"What's for lunch?" asked Ian.

"We ate it already," Jackson answered. "Don't you remember?"

"Oh, yeah."

"And it's good we did," said Krista. "Otherwise our food would be just as soaked as we are. There must have been six inches of water in those canoes."

"Which is exactly the reason," Skyler said with a smile, "that we had our water fight *after* the lunch break, not before. There's a right way and a wrong way to do these things, you know.

"By the way," Skyler continued, "I'm surprised about something. When we spoke of the great clues God built into this world to help us learn about Him, no one mentioned His most amazing creation: people. *Us!*"

Jackson crossed his arms on his chest. "I suppose we are pretty impressive, huh?"

"I agree," Nancie said, closing her eyes. "I can do
so many wonderful things that I couldn't do
if I were a dragonfly, or a fish, or a deer."

"Can you name some of them for us?" Skyler asked.

"Sure," she answered. "I can laugh!" And she did.

"And I can write stories,"
she continued, thinking hard.

"I can do arithmetic problems...

"I can hope and dream about tomorrow...

"And I can *pray.* That's right, I can pray!"

Just then,
a breeze rustled in the willow trees behind them,
and the children watched it blow ripples
across the river.

"Great answers, Nancie!" said Krista. "I never thought of all that. And it's true, isn't it, Captain Skyler?"

"Absolutely," Skyler answered. "Only *people* can do those things Nancie mentioned. The Bible says we're made *in the image of God.* That means God made us a lot like Himself—so we can hope and dream and pray… and lots more.

"For example, God gave each of us a conscience to tell us that some things are good and others are evil. He made us able to choose between one and the other."

"Just think," Krista said. "Right inside me is the proof that God made me!"

"Exactly," said Skyler. "Deep within us, every human being knows there's a difference between right and wrong. And deep down inside, when we're truly honest with ourselves, we know there has to be Someone greater and higher than we are. There has to be Someone who is so much stronger and wiser and better than any human being could ever be.

> **SUPER TRUTH**
> God tells us clearly about Himself in the way that He made _us_!

"We *know* there's a God! And the reason we know it is that God Himself put those feelings inside our hearts!"

Ian stood up and
looked all
around him.
"So the proof
of God is every-
where," he said.
"Outside us.
Inside us.
Everywhere."

He pointed to a dragonfly
hovering in the air not far away.
"And look! I just noticed:
God made dragonflies
in the shape of a cross!"

Nancie stood up beside him. "You're right, Ian. Like
the cross of Jesus!" She turned to Skyler. "Jesus helps us
understand God too, doesn't He?"

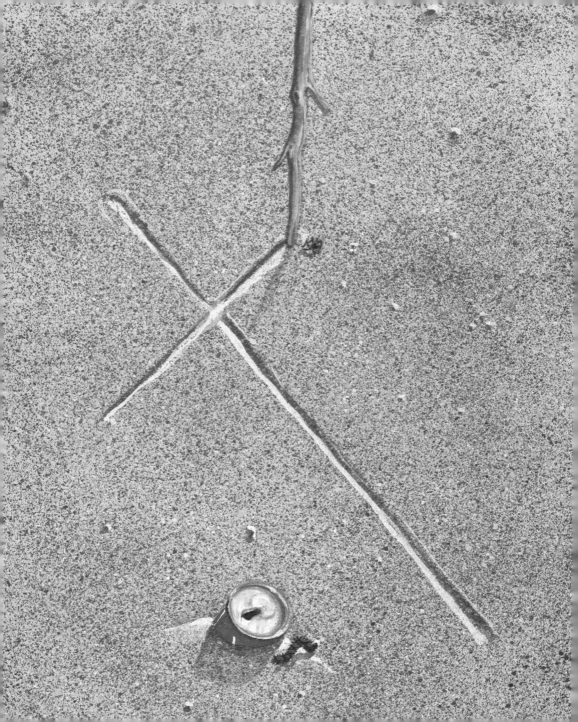

"Does He ever!" Skyler said.

Then he quietly picked up a dry willow stick and drew a simple cross in the sand.

"When Jesus came to earth, it was God's very best way of telling us about Himself.

"God sent Someone to us who was a man, a human being just like us. But that man was also God Himself. In the perfect and loving way that Jesus lived and died, people could see how perfect and loving God is. And in the mighty way that Jesus rose up from the dead, people could see the mighty power of God His Father.

> *Jesus was God's best way of telling us about Himself.*
>
> **SUPER TRUTH**

"In Jesus we learn about God in a far stronger and richer and fuller way than we could ever learn by exploring nature, or looking inside ourselves."

"When Jesus came to earth," Skyler said, "it was God Himself coming down.

"When Jesus *said* something… it was God Himself saying it.

"When Jesus *did* something… it was God Himself doing it.

"In fact, listen to what Jesus told His disciples in John 14:9—

'Anyone who has seen me has seen the Father.'"

"But that was a long time ago," Krista said with a frown.

"Yeah, bummer," said Jackson, as he tossed pebbles into the water. "We weren't there. We didn't get to see Jesus. Does that mean we'll never learn as much about God as the disciples did?"

"Not at all," said Skyler quickly. "You can learn as much as they did—and even more, if you want."

"Are you kidding?" said Ian. "How can that be?"

"Because," Skyler answered, "God has written it all down for you to read. In the Bible! You can read, can't you?"

Ian shrugged. "I'm getting better at it."

"I hope you keep getting better, Ian. And I'll help you anytime you want me to. Because reading the Bible is a *blast,* as Jackson would say. Jesus came to earth and lived the most amazing life! Then He died and rose again, like nothing the world has ever seen.

"And only in the Bible can we hear God telling us all about it."

"Here's something else amazing," said Skyler: "The Bible tells not only *what* happened, but *what it really means*. And not only about Jesus, but also about how the world was made, and how man was created, and all about the most important things that have happened ever since.

"The Bible is the only book that tells us this much about who we really are, and how we should really live...and what happens to us after we die."

"What an incredible gift God has given us in the Bible! Don't you think so?" Skyler asked, while he and the children began launching the canoes back into the river. The afternoon sun was dropping in the sky. It was time to finish their river trip.

"You know, Captain Skyler," said Nancie, "I suppose the Bible really is an incredible gift. But I find it so hard to understand sometimes."

"Yeah," said Jackson. Ian and Krista nodded their heads.

"Well it doesn't *have* to be hard to understand," Skyler said. "And I'd like to show you."

"How?" asked Krista.

Skyler thought for a minute, as both canoes caught the river's main current and pushed ahead through the waters.

"I'll show you in a big way!" he finally answered. "As a matter of fact, I'd like to start tomorrow afternoon by taking all of you for a ride in my brother's helicopter. Does that sound like a good way to do it?"

The children could hardly believe their ears. They shouted, *"YES!"* all at the same time.

QUESTION CORNER

Whatever is true,
whatever is noble,
whatever is right,
...think about
such things.

Philippians 4:8

How is the Bible different from all other books?

What are some different ways in which God tells us about Himself?

What are the MOST IMPORTANT ways in which God tells us about Himself?

Why can we learn so much about God by learning about Jesus Christ?

How can we know about God as well as Jesus' disciples did?

What do you know about dragonflies?

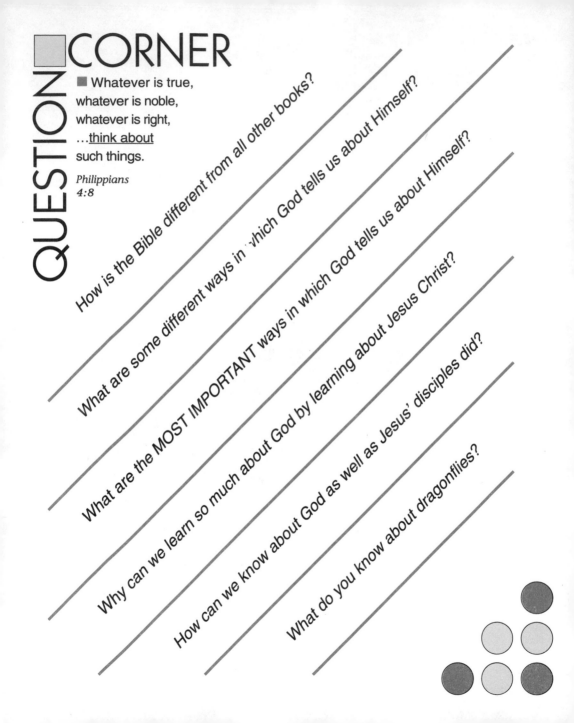

WHAT'S THIS?

The next day when the children's parents dropped them off at the airport, Skyler met them with a book in his hand—a book with a brown leather cover and gold-edged pages.

"Look at this," he said to the children. "What do you call this?"

"The *Bible*," they all answered.

"And what other names do you know for it?"

"The *Scriptures*," said Jackson.

"And *God's Word*," Nancie added.

"You got it," Skyler said. "Three names for the same thing: *Bible, God's Word, Scripture.*

"The word *Bible* means 'book,' and we often call the Bible the 'Book of books.'

"*God's Word,* of course, means anything actually spoken by God.

"And *Scripture* means 'something written.' God's Words have been written down for us so we can read them for ourselves."

A Ride Above
the River

*An Overview
of the Book of Books*

3 The powerful helicopter motor was nonstop noise as Skyler and the children flew away from the city airport. The sound throbbed all through the helicopter's cabin.

"You'll have to shout to be heard!" Skyler told them.

"That's okay," Jackson said. "We like to shout."

"What did you say?" Skyler called out.

"I said," Jackson answered, screaming as loud as he could, *"WE LIKE TO SHOUT!"*

"Got it!" Skyler said with a nod and a grin.

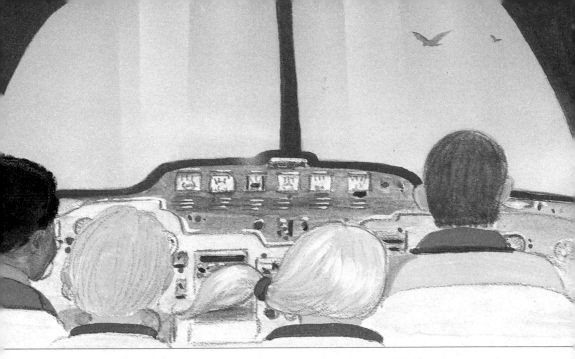

"Captain Skyler!" shouted Krista. "Tell me again where we're going—and why!"

As Skyler answered, his voice was strong and slow so everyone could hear. "There's an old saying that time is like a river. Other things are like a river too. One of them is the Bible.

"Down there's our river—to our left. See it? I'm going to take you to where the river begins, high in the mountains. We'll follow it downstream, and learn how much it and the Bible are alike."

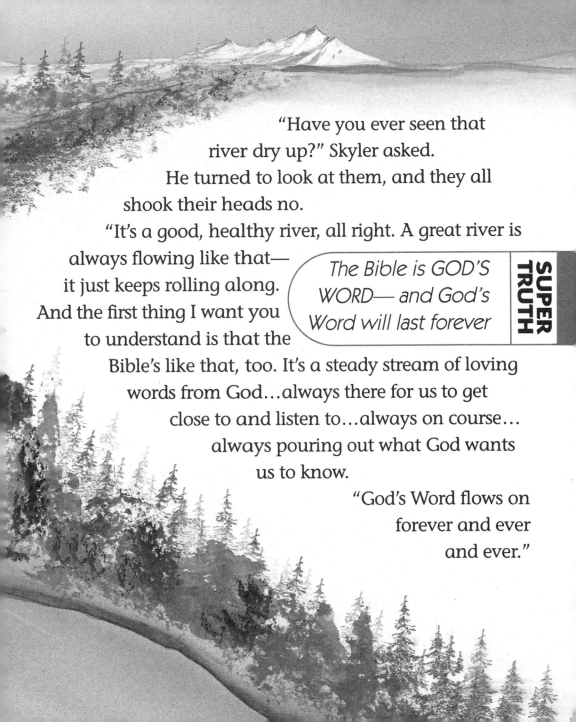

"Have you ever seen that
river dry up?" Skyler asked.
He turned to look at them, and they all
shook their heads no.
"It's a good, healthy river, all right. A great river is
always flowing like that—
it just keeps rolling along.
And the first thing I want you
to understand is that the
Bible's like that, too. It's a steady stream of loving
words from God…always there for us to get
close to and listen to…always on course…
always pouring out what God wants
us to know.

"God's Word flows on
forever and ever
and ever."

> **SUPER TRUTH**
>
> *The Bible is GOD'S WORD— and God's Word will last forever*

"Many long years ago, a man spoke about this in a prayer. It's a prayer we can still read in the Bible, in Psalm 119. Maybe it was a dark night, and the man was alone or afraid. Then he thought about a Bible verse or two, and once again God's Word gave him comfort. So he looked up into the stars, and he heard the truth of God flowing in his heart. And he said,

> O LORD, *your word is everlasting;*
>   *it continues forever in heaven.*

"And catch this: Later in the Bible, in chapter 5 of Matthew, Jesus said that until heaven and earth disappear, the Bible wouldn't lose even the smallest letter, or the tiniest part of a letter.

"The Bible," Skyler shouted, "is here to stay!"

"And since we're thinking about rivers today," Skyler said, "let me tell you about a Happy River, a river that brings joy.

"In Bible times, God had a home called the Temple. It was in Jerusalem—a city which has never had a river. But right there in the Bible, in Psalm 46, you can find a verse that says there's a river in the city of God— in the place where God lives. The verse tells us that the streams of that river bring happiness to the city.

"Now, there's no longer an actual Temple for God in Jerusalem, or anywhere else on earth. God lives in heaven, as He always has, and He also lives in the hearts of all the people on earth who believe in His Son, Jesus Christ."

"So," Jackson asked, "where in the world is that happy river?"

"That's my question too," said Skyler. "And here's my answer: I think Psalm 46 is talking about a river that runs in heaven—but that also reaches down into our hearts."

"What kind of river could that be?" Nancie asked.

"I think it just has to be the River of God's Word," Skyler answered, "coming down from heaven. It flows through the Bible, and flows on forever, always making us glad.

"So when we read the Bible, and listen to it with our hearts, it's like taking a swim in a river of joy—a River of Life. Even though it may not get us wet!" Skyler added, with a special smile for Jackson.

Soon there were mountains in sight, and before long, peaks and valleys were passing right below the helicopter.

"They're beautiful!" Nancie exclaimed.

Ian wasn't looking much at the mountains. He was fascinated by all the pilot's controls and dials spread out before Skyler. What did they all mean? Maybe Skyler could tell him. And maybe, just maybe…

"Captain Skyler," Ian said, as nicely as he could and still be heard above the motor. "If any of us children would like to take a turn being pilot, would you let us?"

Skyler was looking out the window and down. "Well, now," he answered, without turning to Ian, "flying a chopper is no easy job."

"No, sir, I'm sure it isn't—but you could help us, couldn't you?"

Skyler was still looking out. *"There it is!"* he suddenly called. "The place where the river begins.

"Let's go down for a better look!"

4 "Here we are," Skyler said. He let the helicopter hover above a place where water sparkled out of the mountainside. "This is where our mighty river starts, after rising up from deep in the ground."

"The water looks so pure and sweet," said Nancie.

"And the Bible starts out the same way," Skyler said. "On the very first page of it we find a simple truth that rises up pure and clear from deep in the past: It's the great truth that *God made everything.*

"But before I get into that, let me ask all of you some questions. First, the Bible has two parts; what are they?"

"That's easy," said Jackson. "The Old Testament and the New Testament."

"You're right, Jackson. That's an easy one to answer for lots of people. The Bible has a part that's older and a part that's newer. But much more important than *that* is what holds those two parts together.

"Now tell me: Can you have a river without water?"

"Of course not," Nancie answered.

"And you can't have the Bible without God," Skyler went on. "God is absolutely everywhere in the Bible."

"The Bible starts out with these words:
'In the beginning, God...'
"We would never even *have* a Bible if God in His love
had not decided to tell us *in His own words* about
Himself and all that He's done. The Bible is *God's Book*
through and through. Don't forget that! What water is
to a river or an ocean, that's what God is to the Bible.

"And speaking of oceans, here's another question:
How much of the ocean has water in it?"

"All of it!" Ian answered with a laugh.

"That's good to know," said Skyler. "Because in the Old Testament book of Isaiah, there's a Bible verse that tells us something wet and wonderful. It says that after Christ returns to earth as our mighty King, the world will be just as full of the knowledge of God as the ocean is full of water!

Only the Bible can claim to be GOD'S OWN WORDS

SUPER TRUTH

"When that time comes, we'll have a complete understanding of how great our God really is!"

"But for now, let's go back to the beginning. The Bible is not just one book, but *66 different books* all put together into one, and arranged in a certain order: 39 books in the Old Testament, and 27 in the New.

"Does that add up to 66, Krista?"

"It sure does," she answered, in only a second and a half. At school, Krista was the best in her class in arithmetic.

"Now," said Skyler, "to better understand how all these books work together, we can group them into parts. In the Old Testament, the first part is a group of five books, all written by Moses. Sometimes we call this first part 'the Books of Moses.' Sometimes we call it the *Pentateuch,** which is a Greek word that simply means 'five books' or 'five scrolls.' My favorite name for it is the beautiful Hebrew word *Torah,* which means 'law.'

"Let's hear you say that word."

"*Torah,*" said Nancie, rolling the sound off her tongue. "*Torah... Torah...* It *is* beautiful."

* *Pentateuch* is pronounced "Penta-tuke."

39  OLD Testament books

+27  NEW Testament books

---

66 BOOKS IN THE BIBLE

"And who," said Skyler, "can tell me the names of those first five books in the Bible?"

Ian did it: *"Genesis... Exodus... Leviticus... Numbers... and Deuteronomy."*

"Perfect," Skyler answered. "Those are the five books that make up the Torah.

"By the way, the name of the first book, *Genesis,* means 'beginnings.'"

"Sounds like a good place to start," said Jackson.

"There couldn't be a better one," Skyler answered. "In these five books of the Torah, God makes it clear that this world and everything in the entire universe belongs to God. He made it, and He's in charge of it."

Genesis

Exodus

Leviticus

Numbers

Deuteronomy

• • • *K E Y • V E R S E* • • •
The LORD said to Abram (Abraham)…"All
peoples on earth will be blessed through you."
Genesis 12:1-3

"Without God," said Skyler, "there would be no stars, no sun, no moon. There would be no world. And, of course, no people."

"And that," Jackson added, "would mean no Skyler, no Nancie, no Krista, no Ian, no Jackson."

"No anybody!" Skyler agreed.

"Now when God made the first man and woman, their hearts were clean and sweet, like the spring bubbling up from the mountain. But one day Adam and Eve disobeyed God. They *sinned*. And so, for the first time in the world, there was shame. For the very first time there was fear. For the first time ever there was pain and hurting.

"God had made a beautiful world, but now it was as if a terrible black spot had come upon it: the darkness of sin and death."

"God had to punish Adam and Eve for their disobedience—their terrible sin that brought death and hurting into His beautiful world.

"As more people were born, they did more and more wrong things, even though they knew better. They sinned more and more.

"Soon, God had to bring more punishment."

Skyler pointed to the spring. "Way up here, high in the mountains, this stream is terribly close to the storms that come flashing and crashing in the sky. You do *NOT* want to be up here in a storm. If I saw a black cloud coming near right now, I'd get this chopper out of here fast!"

All the children searched the sky in every direction. They were glad they couldn't spot even a gray cloud.

"But the storms that hit this mountain," Skyler said, "are like a gentle breeze compared to the big storm that came in the days of Noah. It was a forty-day storm that flooded the entire earth.

"You've heard that story before, of course. And here in the Torah is where we find out all about it."

"I'm glad that awful storm isn't the end of the story," Nancie said.

"In some ways, Nancie, it was just the *beginning!*" said Skyler. "And right from the beginning, right here in the Torah, God shows us He had a plan to save men and women and boys and girls from their sin.

"You might say that more than anything else, the Torah is all about *God's promises.* God promised Noah, for example, that He would never again send a flood to destroy the earth. God gave us the rainbow in the sky as a sign of that promise.

"Later in the Torah, God chose a good man named

Abraham, and decided to give him special blessings. God promised to give him a huge family, and a beautiful country where his family could live."

"Sounds like a good deal," said Jackson.

"Very," agreed Skyler. "And Abraham didn't doubt God or argue with God. No, *Abraham believed God.* So his family became the people of Israel, and that beautiful country God gave him became the land of Israel.

"Hundreds of years later, Jesus Christ came to live and die to save us from our sin. He would be born into the people of Israel, and He would live and die in the land of Israel—Abraham's land!"

"After Abraham's family became the people of Israel, God gave them laws to help them learn how to please Him. You can read these laws in the Torah. They were rules that told Israel how to worship God in the right way, and how to be kind to one another, especially to people who were poor or who had no family.

"In the Torah, God also taught Israel to give food and animal sacrifices each day to God. These sacrifices showed Israel that someday God would send a Savior to die as a sacrifice for our sins.

"So," said Skyler, "in the Torah, these first five books of the Bible, we see something started that can't stop—something that must keep going, until the full story of Jesus Christ and God's plan for the world is told.

"It's just like that spring down there," Skyler added. "Now that the river has begun, it keeps going down and down. It can't stop until it reaches the sea."

With that, Skyler turned the helicopter to follow the new little river downstream. Ian watched him closely, wanting to learn everything Skyler did at the controls.

How I'd love to pilot a helicopter, Ian thought.

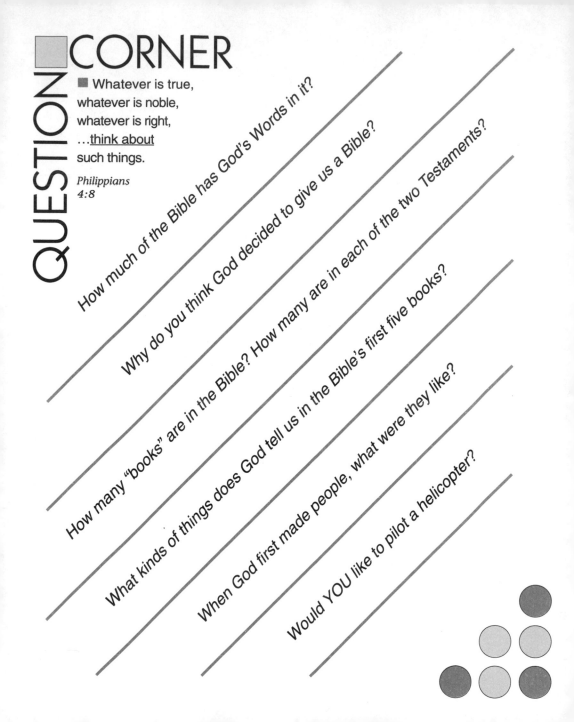

QUESTION CORNER

Whatever is true, whatever is noble, whatever is right, …think about such things.

Philippians 4:8

How much of the Bible has God's Words in it?

Why do you think God decided to give us a Bible?

How many are in each of the two Testaments?

How many "books" are in the Bible?

What kinds of things does God tell us in the Bible's first five books?

When God first made people, what were they like?

Would YOU like to pilot a helicopter?

"BREATHED OUT BY GOD"

When we read the Scriptures, it's as if we could hold out our hand and feel the very breath of the Lord sounding out the words. That's what Paul tells us in his famous passage in 2 Timothy 3:16, one of the greatest verses in the Bible for making us certain that the Bible is truly from God.

And how much of the Bible comes from God in this way? All of it! Paul says, "_All_ Scripture is God-breathed..." Even though God used men like Paul and Moses and David to write the Bible, He made sure that the thoughts and the words were fully His. These men were like the "mouthpiece" that God used to breathe out His Word for you and me and them. Later in the Bible, the apostle Peter said this about the writers of Scripture: "Men moved by the Spirit spoke from God."

5 Skyler saw Ian's eyes watching him closely. "So," said Skyler with a smile. "You'd like to pilot this whirlybird—is that right?"

"Oh, can I?" exclaimed Ian.

"Here's Lesson Number One in Helicopter Piloting," replied Skyler, speaking loud enough so all the children could hear. "Watch me, and listen carefully.

"Do you see all these dials and gauges? They tell me how I'm doing as I fly this thing.

"If something's wrong, these indicators will tell me.

"By the way, they remind me of one of my favorite Bible passages. In the last two verses of 2 Timothy chapter 3, the great apostle Paul said that Scripture is useful for lots of things. And one of them, Paul said, is showing people what's wrong in their lives.

"If my life was this helicopter, then the Bible would be a lot like these gauges, telling me when I need to make changes, to keep from crashing." He passed his hand slowly over all the dials and gauges.

"And of course, once you know something's wrong, you want to *do* something about it. That's true in piloting a helicopter, and it's true in life.

"In those same verses in 2 Timothy 3, Paul said Scripture is useful for correcting our faults and mistakes. He said a person who learns from the Bible has everything he needs to live as he should for the Lord.

"In the same way, right here in these controls, I have everything I need to make this helicopter do what a helicopter should."

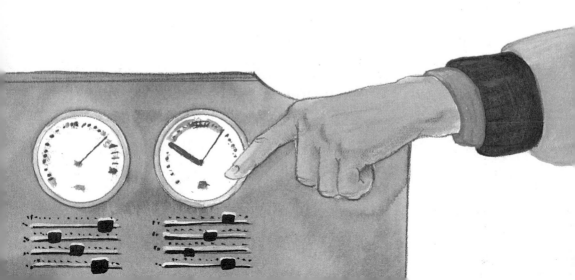

Skyler looked around to make sure he had everyone's attention, then went on: "I have three basic ways to change how we're flying—three controls to correct anything that's wrong. The first is this thing under my left hand. It's called the *collective pitch lever.*

By raising or lowering it, I make the helicopter go up or down. I can also hold the lever in a certain way to make us *hover*—to stay in one place without going up or down.

"I'll raise the lever now, and you'll feel us climbing."

The children could feel the helicopter rising. "Up we go," Skyler said. "It's like what David prayed to the Lord in Psalm 30: 'You lifted me out of the depths.'"

"How does that lever work?" asked Ian.

"It's connected to those big rotor blades spinning around on top of the chopper," answered Skyler, swinging his finger in a circle above his head. "It changes their *pitch*—which means how bent or slanted they are, like the slant you see in the blades of a fan."

"This stick between my knees," Skyler said, "is my second control. It's called the *control column.* I can tilt it forward, backward, or to either side. That makes the helicopter tilt forward, backward, or sideways."

"How?" asked Ian.

"The control column also changes the pitch of the rotor blades," said Skyler, "but in a different way. It can make the pitch greatest when a blade swings toward the back of the helicopter, and that pushes us forward. If the pitch is greatest when the blade passes around to the front, it pushes us backward. The same goes for either side. Here, let's try it."

The helicopter tipped back and forth. Then it swung left and right. "I don't understand how it works," said Nancie, "but it sure is fun!"

"Tons of fun!" said Skyler. "A helicopter can dip and dance in a way that airplanes can't. It makes me think of Psalm 150, which tells us we should praise God with dancing. I like to do it in a helicopter."

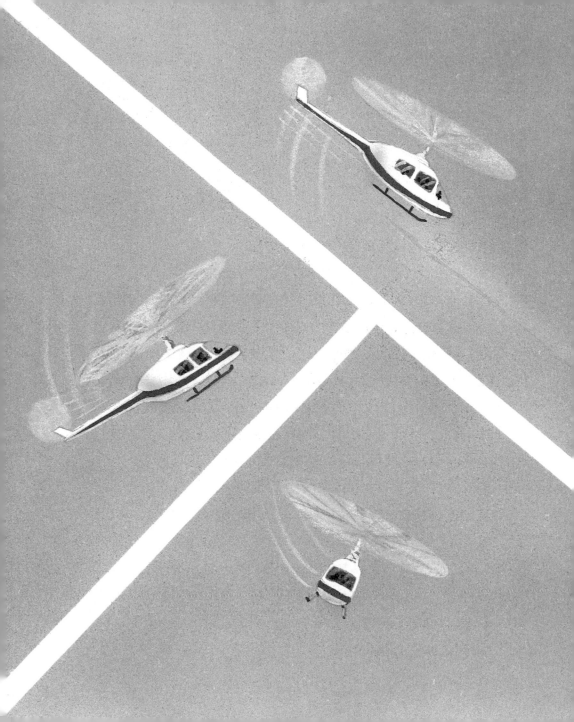

"What's the third control?" asked Jackson.

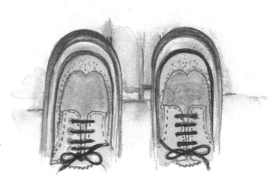

"Look down at my shoes," Skyler said. "Below each foot is a *rudder pedal.* I use them to turn the helicopter without tilting it— the left pedal to turn left, the right pedal to turn right. Like this."

With a touch of Skyler's feet, the helicopter turned to one side, then slowly turned back to the other.

"These pedals change the pitch in the smaller rotor blades that are back on the helicopter's tail," he said, looking at Ian. "That's what changes our direction."

Krista turned to Skyler with a smile. "And I'll bet it reminds you of a Bible verse," she said.

"You know, it does!" replied Skyler. "In Isaiah 30, God talks about the way He guides us in our lives. 'Whether you turn to the right or to the left,' He says, 'your ears will hear a voice behind you saying, "This is the way."' That's a great promise, and we hear that voice most often when we're reading God's Word."

"How?" asked Ian.

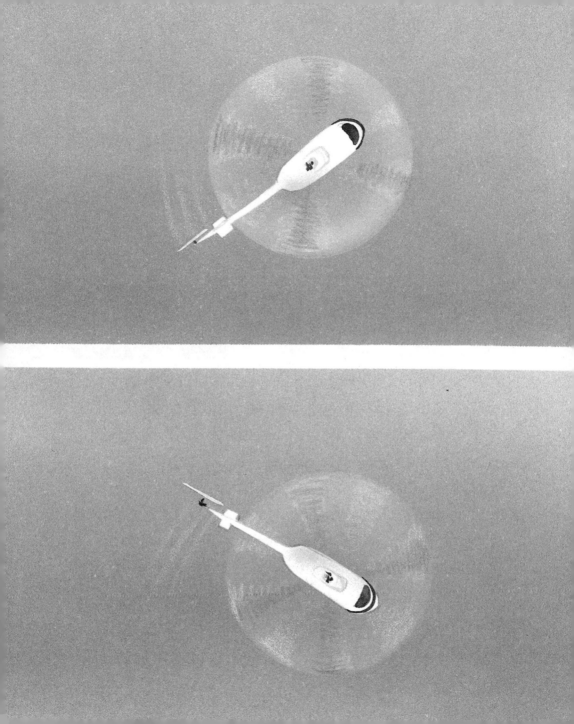

"Let me ask a question," Skyler said. "How do you think a person can get to know the Bible well?"

"You read it and study it," Krista answered, "and you think long and hard about what it means."

"Super answer, Krista. In the Bible, God tells us to love Him with all our minds. He gave us strong minds, and He wants us to put them to work when we open the Bible's covers and look inside. We can all do that, and we all should. BUT…it takes more than brain-power to understand the Scriptures."

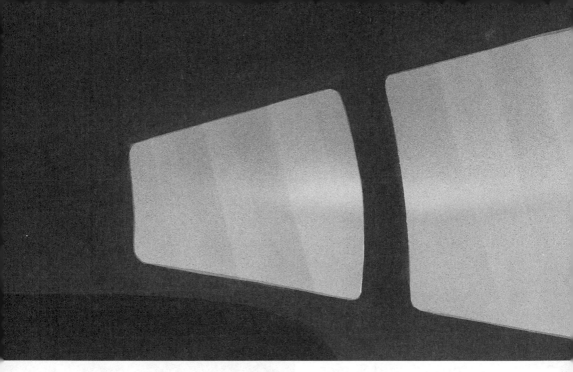

"Like what?" said Krista.

Skyler put his hand on his chest. "Like God's Holy Spirit inside us," he said. "You see, the Bible is God's book, not a human book, and our human minds could never understand it on our own. But the help we need is right here, when we pray and ask God for it.

"You see, God really *wants* us to understand the Bible, so He's given us His Holy Spirit to work in our minds and hearts. The Holy Spirit helps us see the deep truth in the Bible that we would never see otherwise."

"Suppose," said Skyler, "you're in a room full of beautiful treasures. You have two very good eyes, but there's no light in the room. It's completely dark. That means you can't see what's there, no matter how good your eyes are. What you need is *light!*"

"The Bible is full of treasures too," he went on, "and the Holy Spirit within us helps us 'see' those treasures. The Holy Spirit gives us that 'light' in our minds and in our hearts."

Skyler opened his eyes as wide as he could. "Of course," he said, "you also need good 'eyes' to see the treasure, and only a Christian has them. When we believe in Jesus, God gives us the Holy Spirit, and it's like putting on a pair of spiritual 'glasses'—like Jackson's glasses. Then we can see the things we were blinded to before."

"I'm beginning to think," Krista said, "that it's really important to God for us to understand the Bible."

"And why do you think that's so?" Skyler asked.

Krista looked out at a majestic tower of white clouds in the distance, and she thought for a moment. "It must have something to do…with His love for us," she finally said.

Jackson nodded, holding his glasses in his hands. "I think so too."

"Me too," said Skyler. "You know, the more I understand the Bible, the more I love it—and the more I love the One who wrote it, because I know *He loves me.* It makes me want to obey Him with all my heart and soul and mind and strength.

"Lots of Christians will tell you the same thing. The Holy Spirit helps them love God and His Word in this way. He makes us *want* to know His Word and obey it.

"Besides," Skyler said with a nod, "there are some things in life you want to be absolutely, positively sure about. And those things are what the Bible is all about: Where we go after we die, how to live a good life that pleases God, and how to find true love and happiness.

"Say," Skyler said with a whistle, "I think it's time to get back to our river. Down we go!"

6 Below the helicopter now, the narrow river twisted and turned on its way down the mountain toward the sea.

"Do you see how the river zigzags down there?" Skyler called out. "It's a lot like the second big part of the Bible. We call this part the *Old Testament History Books,* and they have some of the most exciting stories in all the Bible, with many of our favorite characters. Joshua, Deborah, Gideon, Ruth, Samuel, David, Jonathan, Elijah, Elisha, Nehemiah, Esther—all these heroes and their brave stories are here in these twelve books of Old Testament history.

"By the time their story starts, millions of people belonged to Israel. We read in these books how they took over the land promised to Abraham. They were a nation now. God gave them their first king, and they built the first Temple for God in Jerusalem.

"But many sad and terrible things also happened in these books. Very often the people turned away from worshiping God, and disobeyed Him. Then God had to discipline them. Many times He sent foreign armies to fight against them.

"Then
the people
would tell God
how sorry they were,"
Skyler continued, "and God
would forgive them. And do you
know what the people always did next?"

"I hope they got smart," said Jackson, "and
quit their sinning."

"That would have been the wise thing to do," said
Skyler. "But instead they turned away from God again,
and even worshiped idols—false gods."

Joshua   Judges   Ruth

1 Samuel   2 Samuel

1 Kings   2 Kings

1 Chronicles   2 Chronicles

Ezra   Nehemiah   Esther

• • • *K E Y • V E R S E* • • •

"Your family and your kingdom will continue forever before me. Your rule will last forever."
God's words to King David in 2 Samuel 7:16

"This happened again and again, and got worse and worse. It was like a sickness. Finally God allowed a foreign army to capture Israel's king, cut out his eyes, and lead him away. They burned down the Temple and all of Jerusalem. They took away most of Israel's people (whom we also call Jews), and forced them to live in captivity in another land. The Jews had lost their king, their land, and their Temple.

"By the way, it's easy to memorize the names of the twelve books that give this history. At the top of the list are the three easy names: *Joshua, Judges, Ruth.*

"In the middle you have the three pairs of names: *1 and 2 Samuel, 1 and 2 Kings, 1 and 2 Chronicles.*

"And then come the three final names: *Ezra, Nehemiah, Esther.* These last books tell what happened after Israel's captivity. The book of Esther is about how God saved the Jews from being destroyed while in the foreign land. Nehemiah and Ezra tell about the Jews returning to Israel to rebuild Jerusalem's walls and the Temple, and getting a fresh new start in Israel.

"So you see, it's a long, long story, with many twists and turns—just like the river below us."

"It sounds like a wild ride for Israel during those years," said Nancie.

"Yeah, wild and woolly," said Jackson with a quick smile. "Especially since they had lots of sheep around."

Skyler missed Jackson's joke, because he was gazing down at the river. "To give you a feel for what a rough-and-tumble story it was," he said, "I'll follow the exact course of the river right here, and we'll take every twist and turn that the stream takes."

He dropped the helicopter down closer to the crooked river. "This may help you," he said, "to imagine what it was like for the people of Israel as they kept going back and forth from good times to hard times during this part of their history."

Skyler veered sharply this way and that, following each crook of the river: left, right, left, right. They also hopped up and down to stay clear of trees and rocks.

Jackson cheered. "Hey, this is like a carnival ride!"

After a few minutes of twisting and turning, Ian was not feeling well at all. "No wonder Israel was sick," he said quietly. But because of the helicopter's loud engine noise, nobody heard him.

Krista noticed him first. "Ian! You look awful!"

Skyler turned and saw him too. "Hey, buddy, I think it's time we landed this machine," he said. "And I know just the place."

Skyler made no more jerky turns. Instead, he smoothly lifted the helicopter up a little further from the river. Then he eased the aircraft away, toward the place he had in mind.

"Now I'm not so sure I'd make a good helicopter pilot," Ian mumbled with a frown. But once again, no one heard him.

■ CORNER

QUESTION

● Whatever is true,
whatever is noble,
whatever is right,
...think about
such things.

*Philippians
4:8*

What are the Scriptures useful for?

What has God done to help us understand the Bible?

Why can't we understand the Bible without this help?

What kinds of things happen in the Old Testament History books?

Why is it important to God that we understand the Bible?

How can YOU get to know the Bible well?

"THE SEED"

DISCOVER
Mark
4:1-20

When the Lord Jesus spoke His famous parable of the seed and the soils, He told the people *twice* to pay careful attention to it. He must have known how easy it would be for us to miss the point of the parable!

Jesus said the "seed" in this parable is God's Word—especially His message about Jesus being our King. This word is like seed which the Lord Himself scatters everywhere over the ground. Though some of it falls where it won't grow—the ground is hard, or rocky, or covered with weeds—other seed falls on good soil, where it takes root and grows up to be a bountiful crop of grain.

Is your heart good soil for God's Word to grow? Do you listen carefully to it, and ask questions in your heart about the true meaning of it? And do you find yourself wanting to do what God tells us to do in His Word?

7 Several minutes later they were all resting on the shore of a wide mountain lake.

"How do you feel, Ian?" Nancie asked.

Now that they were on the ground and relaxing in such a beautiful setting, Ian's sickness had disappeared. But he wasn't smiling yet; he was thinking how their bit of rough riding in the helicopter hadn't bothered anyone except him.

"I feel great," he answered Nancie, while he looked out over the lake. "I wish we had our canoes here. That water is so calm and inviting. And look," he continued,

pointing far away to one end of the lake. "I can see where the river flows into it."

"That's right," Skyler said. He pointed to the opposite shore. "And over there the river flows out again. This lake is really just a part of the river."

"And a very refreshing part," said Krista. She turned to Skyler. "Is this lake like a part of the Bible too?"

"Yep," answered Skyler, "a part that's even more beautiful and refreshing and peaceful than this place is. It's in the very middle of the Bible, and it has five books—we call them *Poetry and Wisdom Books.*"

Job

Psalms

Proverbs

Ecclesiastes

Song of Solomon

• • • *K E Y • V E R S E* • • •

The fear of the LORD is the beginning of
wisdom.... To him belongs eternal praise.
Psalm 111:10

"There's beauty and poetry throughout the Bible," Skyler said, "but especially here. In these books, maybe more than in any other part of the Bible, we learn how important beauty is to God. That's because these books are beautiful not only in what they say, but *how* they say it—in the way they're written. Because of their powerful beauty, these books give us pictures we can remember forever, deep in our minds and hearts."

"What are these five books?" asked Nancie.

"The first is *Job*. It gives us a picture of how to face the terrible hurt that sometimes comes into our lives.

"Next are the *Psalms*. This book gives us a picture of how to love God. In the Psalms, by the way, we find this famous verse that David wrote about the Lord: *'He leads me beside quiet waters.'* Just like this quiet lake!

"Next come the *Proverbs*. They give us a picture of how best to get along with other people.

"The fourth book is *Ecclesiastes,* which gives us a picture of how to find happiness that doesn't go away.

"The last of the five books is the *Song of Solomon,* or *Song of Songs* as it's sometimes called. It's a beautiful picture of the deep love between a husband and a wife."

"Wow!" Jackson said, as he skipped a rock across the smooth-as-glass lake water. "I didn't know the Bible had all of that in it."

"And we're only halfway through," said Skyler.

Nancie also skipped a rock, and said, "My mother and father once told me that they like to read in the Psalms and the Proverbs every day."

Skyler skipped a rock too. "And the same is true for *lots* of Christians, Nancie.

"So often in the Psalms
you can find just the right
words to tell God how you feel—
whether you're afraid, or tired, or happy, or
worried. The Psalms are a reflection of our
hearts, and of God's heart too. The Proverbs, meanwhile, tell us how to be wise—how to do what is right
with our family and friends and neighbors, and with
our leaders, and with our money, and with our bodies,
and in our work, and in our choices, and in our speech
…and on and on."

Skyler reached out and laid his hands on Jackson's
and Ian's shoulders. "And you'll like the fact that the
Proverbs, more than any other book in the Bible, were
written especially with folks your age in mind."

A few minutes later, Skyler and the children took one last look at the quiet lake.

"Remember this view," Skyler said, "and let the memory remind you of the beauty and peace and strength that millions of Christians have found in this part of the Bible. In times of great happiness and times of great sadness, and everything in between, Christians have found in these books a gateway to their hearts, and to God's heart as well."

Skyler looked far away across the water as he continued. "It's been true for Mrs. Brown and me, too.

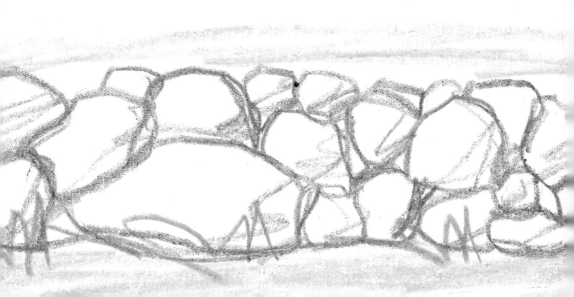

"Someday I'll show you in our journals a few of the verses we've copied from these books, especially Psalms and Proverbs. They were God's special word to us at special times—like the day years ago when we were married, and the day we became parents…and the dark days last fall after our only child was killed…"

With tears in his eyes, he went on. "It's true: Here in these books you can discover the real truth of what David prayed so well in Psalm 29:

The Lord gives strength to his people;
the Lord blesses his people with peace."

They climbed back into the helicopter and took off once more. As they lifted up from the lakeside, the spinning rotor blades made a wild, whooshing wind that whipped up the grass and flowers and trees all around. It quickly spread rough ripples on the water.

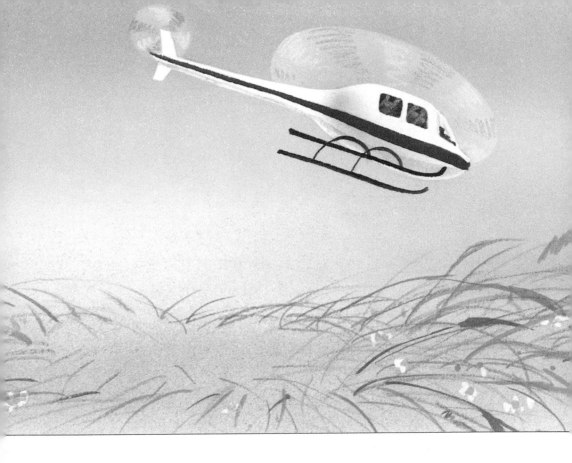

The place didn't seem peaceful anymore.

"The next part of the river," Skyler shouted above the noise, "is the wildest."

Hearing that, Ian pressed his arms against his stomach, and prayed that he wouldn't get sick.

8 Skyler was right. This stretch of the river was full of roaring rapids, deep gorges, and rushing currents. "In this place," Skyler said, "the river is loud, crying out to be heard.

"God wanted to be heard by the people of Israel too. Do you remember when we talked about the twelve Old Testament history books, with their twisting, turning history? We learned how the people of Israel kept sinning in big ways, over and over again, and finally God had to take away their land, their Temple, and their king."

"It makes me wonder," Jackson said, "why God didn't warn them about what would happen if they didn't stop sinning."

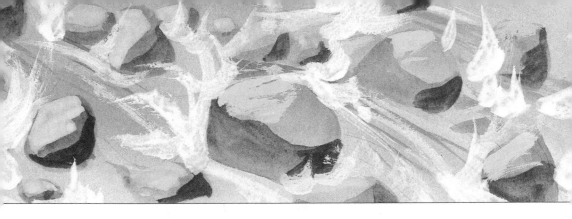

"Good thinking, Jackson," Skyler said. "And that's just the point. God *did* warn them—again and again.

"So many of Israel's people were worshiping idols, fighting against each other, and not caring much whether they treated one another with love and fairness. But some people in Israel did not take part in these sins, and God chose a few of them to be His special messengers. They were to warn all the people of Israel about the consequences of their sin.

"These few messengers were the men God chose to call the people back to the Lord. They were called *prophets.* And the books they wrote—the messages they received from the Lord, and which we can still read today in the Bible—are called *Prophecy.*"

Isaiah

Jeremiah

Lamentations

Ezekiel

Daniel

• • • *K E Y • V E R S E* • • •

Those who hope in the Lord will renew their
strength. They will soar on wings like eagles...
Isaiah 40:31

"The prophets were able to speak the word of the Lord to the people because God brought them very close to Himself. They heard His very words, and God let them see what other people could not see.

"It's as if the spiritual eyes He gave them were as keen and as powerful as the eyes of an eagle.

"Each of these books by the Prophets is named for the prophet who wrote it—except for the book of Lamentations, which was written by the prophet Jeremiah.

"The books of Old Testament Prophecy are divided into two groups," Skyler explained. "The first group has five books. They're sometimes called the *Major Prophets,* not because they're more important than the other prophets, but because their books are mostly larger. These five books are *Isaiah, Jeremiah, Lamentations, Ezekiel, and Daniel.*

"Isaiah and Jeremiah wrote their books before the nation of Israel went into captivity in the land of Babylon. Ezekiel and Daniel were written while the Jews were still captives in Babylon."

"There are twelve other books of Old Testament Prophecy. These last twelve books are sometimes called the *Minor Prophets,* because their books are shorter.

"And I know some clues that may help you learn these twelve names. I'll start at the bottom of the list: The last one of these twelve, *Malachi,* is the very last book in the Old Testament, and it starts with the same letter as the first book of the New Testament—Matthew. So just remember: <u>M</u>alachi, <u>M</u>atthew."

"*Mmmmmmmm,*" said Jackson.

"Yeah! Then, right before Malachi are two pairs of books that begin first with an <u>H</u> and then with a <u>Z</u>: *Habakkuk* and *Zephaniah,* then *Haggai* and *Zechariah.*

"And right before those, in the exact middle of this list, are two books, *Micah* and *Nahum,* that begin with <u>M</u> and <u>N</u> — which also happen to be the exact middle letters in our English alphabet.

"Now then, all that's left to learn on this list are the first five books: *Hosea, Joel, Amos, Obadiah,* and *Jonah.*

"So," Skyler asked, "does that sound easy?"

"Not super easy," said Krista, "but we'll work on it. I sure like the sound of those names."

Hosea   Joel   Amos

Obadiah   Jonah

Micah   Nahum

Habakkuk   Zephaniah

Haggai   Zechariah

Malachi

• • • *K E Y • V E R S E* • • •

Come back to the LORD your God....He has great
love. He would rather forgive than punish.

Joel 2:13

"There's one thing more I would like to tell you about these books," Skyler said, as he lifted the helicopter away from the loud rapids and headed farther downstream. "Since the Lord allowed the prophets to see into the future, it was as if they were looking through a huge telescope across all time. They could see far beyond the terrible destruction and captivity that Israel soon would be facing from enemies. Far into the future, the prophets saw some amazingly *good* things for God's people. God gave them great and wonderful promises of these good things to come.

"We can read about all these promises and good things here in the Prophets, more than in any other part of the Old Testament. They all had to do with a special Man. As the prophets listened to what God told them, they gave this Man names like these: *'Servant of the Lord, Immanuel, Wonderful Counselor, Mighty God, Everlasting Father,* and *Prince of Peace.'*

"Hundreds of years before this Man actually came, God let the prophets see that He would be born in the town of Bethlehem, and would have a virgin for His mother. They understood that He would suffer and die for the sins of the world. But then He would overcome death itself. This Man is what the next and most exciting part of the river is all about.

"And I think you can probably guess just who He is."

QUESTION CORNER

Whatever is true,
whatever is noble,
whatever is right,
…think about
such things.

*Philippians
4:8*

What are the five Wisdom & Poetry books?

Which book tells us especially how to love the Lord?

Which book tells us especially how to get along with other people?

What kinds of things does God say through the Prophets?

Which five books make up the "Major Prophets"?

What is a prophet?

"RAIN AND SNOW"

God's Word is not only like seed that grows and becomes a good crop—but it's also like the moisture that falls from the sky to make those crops grow!

The prophet Isaiah tells us what the Lord Himself says about it:

Rain and snow fall from the sky.
They don't return
without watering the ground.
They cause the plants to sprout and grow.
And the plants make seeds
for the farmer.
And from these seeds
people have bread to eat.

The words I say do the same thing.
They will not return to me empty.
They make the things happen
that I want to happen.
They succeed in doing
what I send them to do.

God's Word can make things happen!

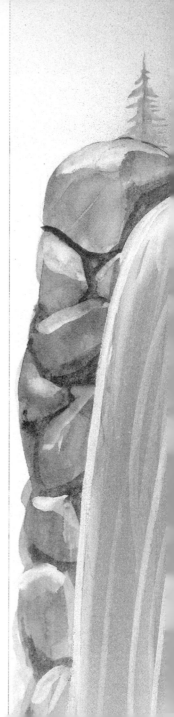

9 Ahead of them, the children saw a place where the river seemed to simply drop out of sight. The helicopter swooped over the place, and they saw what was really there: The river tumbled over the edge of a cliff and became a towering, thundering waterfall. The foaming, falling river sparkled like a million diamonds in the sunlight.

"*AWESOME!*" Jackson shouted. But he couldn't even hear the word himself, because the sound of the crashing waters was so deafening.

Skyler, with his left hand on the collective pitch lever, lowered them down in front of the falls. The helicopter dropped slowly beside the plunging waters.

No one even tried to say anything now—not only because of the noise, but also because it seemed impossible to find words to describe what they were seeing and hearing.

There *were* words in Skyler's mind, however—words he remembered from long ago. When Skyler was a boy, his father had brought him here for the first time, and taught him this phrase from Psalm 42:

> *Deep calls to deep*
> *in the roar of your waterfalls.*

"The roar calling out from a waterfall reminds me of something," Skyler's father had told him. "And this is it: The feelings deep in my heart call out, and God hears them deep in *His* heart. It works the other way too: The deep love in God's heart calls out to me, His child, and I hear it deep inside me.

"*Deep calls to deep.* Even when we don't have a waterfall close by, we can still hear the call, just by reading God's Word with a listening heart."

Skyler let the helicopter hover not far from the foot of the falls. Here the water pounded down onto rocks, and crashed through the surface of the lower river. The noise here was deeper and louder than ever. A misty spray was everywhere.

After several moments, Skyler lifted the helicopter away from the falls so they could all hear each other speak.

"What do you think would happen," he asked, "if we went over this waterfall in the canoes we were riding in yesterday?"

Jackson whistled and said, "Goodbye, life."

"Certain death," said Ian.

"For sure," agreed Krista. The children shuddered just to think of it.

"In the same way," Skyler said, "it was certain death for Jesus to come here to earth. He was God Himself, the One through whom all life was created. Yet *He came here to die.*

"Every man and woman and boy and girl on earth had become a slave to sin and death. Jesus came to die for them, to take their death upon Himself. Otherwise, He knew, there was no possible way we could live forever with God.

"The world was lost and dying. And the Lord Jesus Christ, the Son of God, left heaven to come here and save the world."

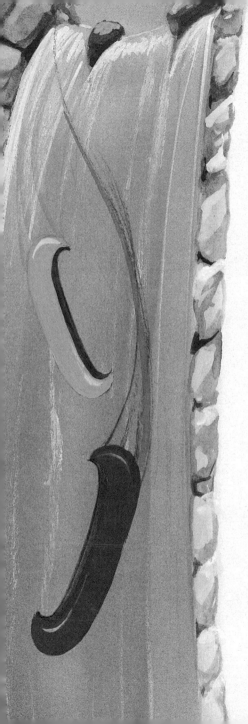

"I see what you mean," said Nancie. "It's like this waterfall. The water starts so very high, then falls so very far. That's what it was like for Jesus to leave His home in heaven and come to earth. Just think: To be God, and yet be born in a little stable in a little town as a little baby in a poor little family!"

"And then," Jackson added, "to grow up and have to be killed like a criminal, even though He never did anything wrong..." Jackson shook his head in amazement.

"What a story," said Krista.

"And that story," Skyler said, "is told in the four books of the Bible that we call the four *Gospels*."

New Testament GOSPELS: 4 Books

Matthew

Mark

Luke

John

• • • *K E Y • V E R S E* • • •

"The Son of Man did not come to be served, but to serve, and to give his life as a ransom for many."
Jesus' words about Himself in Mark 10:45

"By the way, how do you like this part of the river?" Skyler asked.

"It's my favorite by far!" Ian said.

"Yeah," Krista said. "So exciting. Breathtaking!"

"It's my favorite part too," Skyler said. "And just as this waterfall is the most amazing and exciting part of the river, so the Gospels are the most amazing and exciting part of the Bible. For this is where we see the mighty God Himself coming down to earth.

"Maybe you already know the names of these four books. Each of you try to name one for me. Which one of the gospels is first, Nancie?"

"Matthew," she answered.

"Then Mark," offered Ian.

"And then John," Jackson said.

Krista looked puzzled. "Oh, Jackson, I think you're mistaken. I believe Luke is third, and then John."

"She's right," said Ian.

Nancie nodded too.

"I knew that," Jackson said with a grin. "I just wanted to see if all of *you* did."

Skyler laughed at Jackson, then went on: "In each of these four books, someone different tells the story of Jesus' life, and His death and resurrection. All of these writers—Matthew, Mark, Luke, and John—were very close to Jesus when He lived on earth, or else learned about Him from others who were close to Jesus."

"But why does the Bible give the story four times," asked Krista, "instead of just once?"

"One reason," Skyler answered, "is that each of the writers tells us the story of Jesus in his own special way —just as each of you four children would tell the story of this helicopter trip or yesterday's canoe trip in *your* special way."

"I've got it," said Jackson. "We learn a lot more… since we learn from all four!"

"That's it," Skyler said. "And think about this: The Gospels are the story of how God came to *earth*—and four is a number that has a lot to do with the earth. We sometimes talk about the 'four corners' of the world, and the 'four winds' that come from earth's four directions—north, south, east, and west. We also speak of earth's four seasons—winter, spring, summer, fall.

"The number three, meanwhile, often symbolizes God. For example, the Bible speaks of the three Persons of God: the Father, the Son, and the Holy Spirit. We call them the 'Trinity,' which means 'three.'

"In the Gospels, the Son of God becomes a Man and comes to earth—which means three joins with four. If you add three and four together you get seven, which in the Bible is a number that often means *perfect* and *complete*. In the Gospels, when Jesus comes to the world, it opens up the way for you and me to be perfect and complete."

Below the waterfall, the river spread out wide and strong. Skyler piloted the helicopter away from the falls and down this new stretch of the stream.

"Just as this waterfall is the beginning of what is practically a new river, so these four Gospels are the start of what is almost a new Bible. All the books we looked at earlier were in the Old Testament. From the Gospels on, all the books are in the New Testament.

"After the four Gospels, the next book is a part of the New Testament all by itself. It's called *Acts*. The book of Acts begins with Jesus going back to heaven after He rose up from the dead. But in the rest of the book we can still see His life in the lives of His disciples. They were alive with the mighty power of the Holy Spirit."

"What exactly is the Holy Spirit?" Ian asked.

"Great question, Ian. First of all, the Holy Spirit is a 'Who,' not a 'What.' The Holy Spirit is God Himself living inside those who believe in Jesus.

"Before Jesus died, He promised His disciples that He would send His Spirit to live inside them. And that's exactly what happened after He rose up from the dead and then went back to heaven.

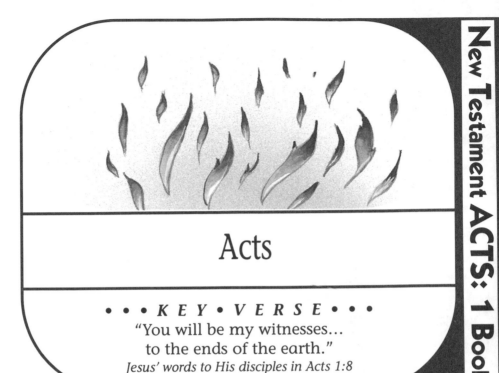

Acts

• • • **K E Y • V E R S E** • • •

"You will be my witnesses...
to the ends of the earth."
Jesus' words to His disciples in Acts 1:8

"The Holy Spirit inside the disciples made them bold and brave. In the book of Acts, they left Israel and began taking the good news of Jesus all around the world. And with the Holy Spirit inside you and me, *we* can be bold and brave too—wherever God sends us.

"Hey," said Skyler, looking over one shoulder, "I see rain clouds off to the west."

"You know," Skyler said, "often when the rain pours down, I think of one of my favorite verses in Acts. Simon Peter was preaching, and he remembered these words from Joel, one of the Old Testament prophets:

'In the last days, God says,
I will pour out my Spirit on all people....
I will pour out my Spirit in those days,
and they will prophesy.'

"In the Book of Acts, God's Spirit came pouring down on His people like a big summer rain. And still today, God freely gives us His Spirit to refresh us and help us grow."

10 "Hey, look!" shouted Jackson, glancing down. "There's where we were yesterday!"

"Yeah, in the canoes!" Ian said. "I can see where we had the water fight!"

The helicopter had now flown several miles from the waterfall. The river below was wide and rich here, flowing through fruitful farmlands. Skyler had explained that the next part of the Bible was like that too: rich and fruitful.

"It's made up of 21 *Letters*," Skyler said, "and they teach us *what* to believe and *how* to live. They make the story of the Gospels even richer for us."

"How's that?" Jackson asked.

"Well," Skyler explained, "the Gospels tell us *what Jesus did,* while the Letters tell us *what that means for you and me.* That's it in a nutshell."

"Oh, that reminds me," Krista said. She reached for a paper bag at her feet, opened it, and offered its contents to the others.

"Peanuts, anyone?"

They all had some.

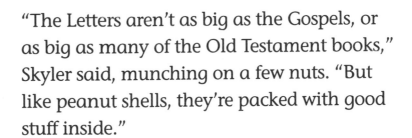

"The Letters aren't as big as the Gospels, or as big as many of the Old Testament books," Skyler said, munching on a few nuts. "But like peanut shells, they're packed with good stuff inside."

Romans

1 Corinthians 2 Corinthians

Galatians Ephesians

Philippians Colossians

1 Thessalonians 2 Thessalonians

1 Timothy 2 Timothy

Titus Philemon

• • • K E Y • V E R S E • • •

"Just as you received Christ Jesus as Lord,
continue to live in him."
Colossians 2:6

"How did someone's letters become part of the Bible?" Krista asked, when the bag of nuts was empty.

"And who wrote the letters, anyway?" Ian said.

"And who were the letters to?" asked Jackson.

"All great questions, guys," Skyler said. "Let's see, where to begin…" He thought for a moment, then said:

"These Letters are arranged in the Bible according to who wrote them. The first 13 Letters are all by Paul. Some of them he wrote while he was in prison."

Krista gasped. "What was he doing in prison?"

"That's a long and fascinating story," answered Skyler. "We read much of it in the book of Acts. Paul was falsely accused of wrong by religious leaders, and was kept in prison by the Romans for a long time.

"Meanwhile he kept writing letters. His first nine letters in the Bible were written to Christians in different places: one to the *Romans* who were Christians; then two to the *Corinthians;* one each to the *Galatians,* the *Ephesians,* the *Philippians,* and the *Colossians;* and then two letters to the *Thessalonians.*

"The next four letters were written by Paul to men who were Christian workers—two to his helper *Timothy,* one to his helper *Titus,* and one to his friend *Philemon.*"

"What about the other eight letters?" asked Nancie. "Who wrote them?"

"Actually, Nancie, we don't know for sure who wrote the first of the eight letters—the letter to the *Hebrews*, a book that probably tells us more about faith than any other book in the Bible. But each of the other letters is named for the man who wrote it: First, *James;* then two letters by *Peter,* and three by *John,* and finally one by *Jude.* Peter and John, you remember, were on Jesus' first team of 12 apostles. And the men who wrote the letters of James and Jude were probably Jesus' brothers.

"Like the ones Paul wrote, all these letters were written to churches and Christian workers. These Christians sometimes felt like sheep among wolves. They faced difficult problems and questions, and needed encouragement—just as Christians do today. The men who wrote these letters were God's messengers with God's wise answers for all who would read them. That's why these letters are still so rich and powerful for you and me, hundreds of years later."

"What kind of questions and problems did they write about?" Jackson asked.

Hebrews

James

1 Peter   2 Peter

1 John   2 John   3 John

Jude

• • • **K E Y • V E R S E** • • •

"Grow in the grace and knowledge of our
Lord and Savior Jesus Christ."

2 Peter 3:18

"Here's a sample," said Skyler, "and as I mention these questions, think about whether you've ever asked them yourself:

- *How can I be a Christian in a world that has so many bad things and bad people in it?*
- *How should I treat the people around me — those who are Christians, and also those who are not?*
- *How does Jesus help me live my life? How can He change me to be a better person?*
- *And what does it really mean for Jesus to be my LORD and my SAVIOR?"*

Skyler saw the children silently nodding their heads. Then he continued:

"As the writers of the New Testament Letters answer these questions, they remind us again and again—just like Jesus did—that God is our loving Father. Not only did He create you and me and the world around us, but by sending us His Son Jesus, He made it possible for us to be *new creations*, living in love with God forever.

"That's why," Skyler continued, "I like to think of these books as personal letters from God to you and me. Like this:

"'Dear Skyler, Dear Nancie, Dear Ian,
Dear Jackson, Dear Krista…

"Please read what I've written here, and keep
My words in your heart. Then you'll know and
understand how much I will always care for you.

Love, God.'"

Nancie had tears in her eyes. "Oh, Captain Skyler, that's beautiful," she said.

"Yeah, that's neat," said Jackson. "These books of the Bible just seem to get better and better. How many more are there?"

"Only one more," Skyler said. "And it's a thriller. Hold on to your seats," he shouted. "We're heading for the edge of tomorrow!"

Skyler lifted the helicopter higher and gave it more speed. Down below, the children could see the rich, wide river spreading out ahead of them.

But in the distance, the picture changed. There on the horizon, something even bigger was waiting for them.

QUESTION CORNER

Whatever is true,
whatever is noble,
whatever is right,
...think about
such things.

*Philippians
4:8*

Why did Jesus Christ come down to this world?

What are the names of the four Gospels? What are they about?

Why did God give us four Gospels instead of just one?

What do we learn about the Holy Spirit from the book of Acts?

Who wrote most of the New Testament Letters?

What are the Letters about?

"ALIVE AND WORKING"

"Ouch!"

We might feel like saying that when God's Word goes straight to our heart to show us a wrong attitude, or a sinful action we're guilty of.

When we read Hebrews 4:12, we can see why God's Word can often hurt. This is one of the most powerful pictures in all the Bible. It tells us that God's Word *"is alive and working. It is sharper than a sword sharpened on both sides. It cuts all the way into us, where the soul and the spirit are joined. It cuts to the center of our joints and our bones. And God's word judges the thoughts and feelings in our hearts."*

God's Word goes in deep. It can find a spot of evil within us, no matter how deeply we've tried to hide it.

There is no such thing as a secret from God!

11 Ian saw it first. "The ocean!" he shouted, when it was still far off. "There it is… Look!"

Under the day's sunny sky, the sea was sparkling blue. Skyler brought the helicopter over the place where the river flowed into it.

"As you can see down there," Skyler said, "the river, in a way, never ends. It becomes the ocean, whose waters flow around the earth in a never-ending circle.

"So we won't stop here!" he added. With a burst of speed, he flew the helicopter right out over the ocean.

"Wow!" said Ian, looking out over the waters. "You can see forever!" He turned to Skyler. "Let's just keep going," he said.

Skyler laughed. "I'm afraid we'd run out of fuel before we found a place to land. Forever's a long way, you know.

"But if you really want to see forever, the best place to look is the last book in our Bible: *Revelation*. In Revelation, it's as if God drew back a curtain so we can all see clearly our forever-future."

"And what do we see there?" asked Krista.

"Ahhh, so very much!" Skyler answered. "More than words can really describe. In fact, Revelation is written in a sort of picture-language. It's running over with exciting pictures you can fill your imagination with. It reads like a dream…because it *is* a dream, really. And someday it will be a dream-come-true."

"A dream?" said Jackson. "What do you mean?"

"Revelation," answered Skyler, "was written for us by the apostle John when he was an old man. The Christians in those days were being attacked by the enemies of God, and John himself was their prisoner on a rugged little island called Patmos.

"One Sunday, there on Patmos, the Lord gave him a vision—a dream. John heard a loud voice that sounded like a trumpet. The voice told him to write down what he was seeing in the vision.

"John turned to look at whoever was speaking to him—and there before his eyes was the Lord Jesus Himself in glory, His face as bright as the sun. John fell at Jesus' feet in fear, but Jesus told him not to be afraid.

"In the rest of the dream John saw amazing and wonderful things. And he wrote them down for us to read and understand and obey."

Skyler paused, and quietly rubbed his chin.

"Oh, please don't stop there," said Nancie. "What else did John see?"

"One thing he saw" Skyler said, "was the last great victory of good over evil. A total, absolute victory.

Revelation

• • • *K E Y • V E R S E* • • •

"Behold, I am coming soon!"
Jesus' words in Revelation 22:12

"John saw for sure that God has a plan to destroy evil once and for all—not only the power of evil, but even the very existence of evil."

"AND," said Skyler with a whistle, "what's even more exciting is that John saw Jesus Himself leading us in that victory at the end of all time.

"The New Testament began with Jesus coming to earth the first time. Here in Revelation, the New Testament ends by showing us how Jesus will come again—not as a baby this time, but as a mighty King, the greatest Hero ever.

"In Revelation, more than anywhere else in the Bible, we see how great Jesus Christ is. Revelation uses more different names and titles for Jesus than any other book.

"Just listen, kids, to all these names and titles of your King and mine:

"Faithful and True Witness,
Firstborn from the Dead,
Ruler of the Kings of the Earth,
the Alpha and the Omega,
the Almighty,
Son of Man,
Son of God,
the First and the Last,
the Living One,
the Amen,
Ruler of God's Creation,
Lion of the Tribe of Judah,
Root and Offspring of David,
the Lamb,
King of Kings,
Lord of Lords,
the Word of God,
and the Bright Morning Star.

"Jesus will be in every
way the kind of King we all
want to serve and worship."

"John saw something else we all long for: *Heaven*. More than any other part of the Bible, Revelation is our book of heaven. John saw that everything is always new there. Heaven is pure and beautiful and dazzling bright, like a bride in her wedding gown. John saw that God wipes away every tear in heaven—there is no more crying or hurting. John saw heaven as a shining city on a mountain great and high, with walls and gates sparkling like jewels, and streets of pure, clear gold. It's a place where there's never any darkness, and where all doors are open.

"And there in the center of the greatest street in heaven, flowing from God's throne, is the River of Life. At any spot along the river, on either side, you can find the Tree of Life, always with fruit on it—a new crop of fruit every month.

"All this, John saw in his dream. So Revelation gives us our greatest hope ever. But Revelation is also a book of warnings. Jesus tells His people not to give in to evil, and to stay strong, or else they will miss His great rewards. Jesus tells us to get rid of the sin in our lives, and to love Jesus as our first love."

"We spoke earlier," Skyler continued, "about the number 7. In the Bible that number means *perfect, complete.* Revelation is the book that brings all the Word of God to completion, and John's dream in Revelation is filled with sevens: 7 golden candlesticks, 7 stars, 7 trumpets, 7 lamps, 7 letters to 7 churches, 7 judgments...on and on. Revelation is like the Bible's crown or its finishing touch. It's like the roof on a house, or the frame around a picture, or the hood of a snowsuit, or the golden crust of a cherry pie.

"Revelation is to the Bible what the ocean is to a flowing river..."

12 Without the children even realizing it, Skyler had slowly brought the helicopter back around toward the river. They were leaving the ocean behind.

"Well now," Skyler said, "I'm going to ask you a question, and on our way back I'd like you to think very carefully before answering. Here it is: What do you think about the Bible now?"

The children thought for a long time.

Skyler was bringing the helicopter closer to the city airport, where their trip would end. Ian was the first to speak up: "I have an answer to your question," he said.

"Good, let's hear it," Skyler said with a smile.

"Actually," Ian said, "I guess it's more of a decision than an answer: I'm sure now that the Bible is God's Word. And it's so good and so important—and so exciting, too—that no matter how hard it might be to understand sometimes, I promise I'll try to keep reading it and studying it all my life."

Skyler quietly nodded his head. Down below, he could see the helicopter landing pad at the airport. "Does anyone else want to say anything?" he asked.

"I agree with Ian," Nancie said.

"Me too," said Krista.

"I couldn't have said it better myself," Jackson agreed.

"That's a wise decision, Ian—and all of you," Skyler said. "You know, the Bible really wasn't meant by God to be an *easy* book. But if you truly want to know and love and obey the Scriptures, there is nothing that can stop you. God Himself will help you do it.

"That's why the most important next step is to ask God for His help. As we talked about before, we can't truly understand the Bible without the Holy Spirit. In fact, why don't we all pray together right now, and ask for His help. Jackson, will you please lead us in prayer?"

"Sure, Skyler," Jackson said. He bowed his head and cleared his throat.

> "Dear Lord," he prayed, "we want to love and obey what You tell us in Your Bible. All four of us—all five of us, that is, Skyler too—we all want to understand the Bible better and better. Please use Your Holy Spirit in our hearts to help us do just that, because we can't do it by ourselves.

"Thank You, Lord.
You know and I know that we'll be glad
and forever grateful for Your help.
In Jesus' holy name,
Amen."

"Let me ask you another question," Skyler said. "Just suppose that after we land this chopper down there, we hear horrible news: While we were up in the air, God's enemies invaded our city. They arrested anyone who admitted that he or she believed in Jesus. In fact, as soon as we stepped out from the helicopter, the enemies met us, took all five of us away, and threw us into prison.

"Now, here's my question: What do you think is the worst possible thing this enemy could try to do to us?"

"I can think of lots of awful things," Jackson said, "but I'd like to know what you think, Skyler."

"Yeah," said Nancie. They were descending toward the landing pad now, and the children were looking down, trying to spot any enemy soldiers.

"Since our trip's nearly over," Skyler said, "I won't make you tell me your answers first. Here's mine: I think the worst thing they could do would be to keep us from thinking about God's Word—to keep us from meditating on Bible verses, to keep us from treasuring them in our hearts and hearing God's voice speak to us through the words, giving us hope and courage.

"I don't see any enemy soldiers below us, but lots of other things down there can keep us from meditating on the Scriptures—like watching too much TV or listening to radio music all the time, or being too busy to read the Bible, or filling our minds with harmful thoughts. *Those* enemies are *real.*"

Skyler slowly dropped the helicopter down to the pad. He checked his controls, then he turned off the motor. The quietness sounded strange after so much noise for so long.

Skyler turned to the four children.

"Here's a fun assignment for you," he said. "Read Psalm 119 in the Bible. It's the longest chapter in Scripture, but stick with it, and I'm sure you'll find something that grabs your attention. I won't tell you what it's about. Just read it, and then draw a picture on paper of something in that psalm that means a lot to you. In a few days, the next time we're together, we'll look at our pictures and talk about the psalm. Okay?"

"Sounds fun," Krista said.

Jackson nodded. "Hey, I'm finally getting hooked on the Book! You know, I could tell from the way my Dad loves reading the Bible that there had to be something to it. I figured that someday I'd understand... Maybe that someday is finally here! Man, will my Dad ever be glad!"

Skyler bent over to open the door. "Say, let's go thank my brother for letting us use his helicopter!"

"Let's do it!" said Jackson.

■ CORNER
QUESTION

■ Whatever is true,
whatever is noble,
whatever is right,
…think about
such things.

*Philippians
4:8*

What is the book of Revelation like?

What does Revelation tell us about heaven?

What kind of warnings are in the book of Revelation?

What do you think is the worst thing an enemy could do to you?

What promise did Ian make to Skyler?

What did Jackson pray?

"LIKE FIRE...
AND LIKE A HAMMER"

DISCOVER
Jeremiah
23:29

In the time of the prophet Jeremiah, many smooth-talking "false prophets" said they spoke the Words of God, but they were only lying.

Jeremiah was truly a prophet of God, and the Lord told him what His Word is really like: *"'Is not my word like fire,' declares the LORD, 'and like a hammer that breaks a rock in pieces?'"*

Like no other book, the Holy Bible has *power.* God's Word is like the fire in the furnaces where gold and silver are put to make them pure. The Bible can burn away the unclean thoughts and desires in our hearts.

And His Word can hit hard like a hammer, with the power to crush our sinful pride. The Bible is not a storybook to merely entertain us, but the powerful Word of God for cleaning and changing us.

Climb a Tree with Me

*Who the Bible
Is All About*

13 Up in an oak tree, Nancie and Krista heard the voice of Mrs. Jordan, their good friend and neighbor, calling out from below: "What do you see on that branch right above you there?"

"Beautiful leaves," Nancie shouted, looking around.

"What else?" came the old woman's voice again.

At Nancie's side, Krista looked straight above her head, then called out, "I see a huge spider web—and the spider, too!" She raised her head to get a closer look.

Nancie and Krista had gone this morning to Mrs. Jordan's house to tell her about their canoe trip and helicopter ride—and also about their adventure of getting ac-quainted with the Bible. Then the three of them decided to come here, to their fa-vorite place in South Hills Park. They called this old oak "The Tower Tree." It stood so tall and big and alone on an otherwise empty hill.

"I doubt that spider will hurt you," Mrs. Jordan called out. "After all, he's on the Mercy Limb."

Krista looked at Nancie, and said quietly, "The *Mercy Limb?* What do you think she's talking about?"

Mrs. Jordan spoke again, with a smile: "And you're standing on the Love Limb. So don't be unkind to that spider!"

" Mrs. Jordan," Krista said, "what do you mean by 'Mercy Limb' and 'Love Limb'?"

Mrs. Jordan gave them a wink: "One Sunday afternoon—years ago, when I was just big enough to climb this tree—my friends from Sunday school and I came here to play. We decided to name all the big limbs on this tree. And for names, we chose all of God's *attributes* which we were learning about in Sunday school."

"*Attributes?* What does that mean?" asked Krista.

"I know it's a strange word," said Mrs. Jordan, "but I don't have a smaller one that will do. An attribute is like an ingredient listed on a candy bar wrapper or a cereal box, except that an attribute is something that's inside a *person*. It's what that person is like."

Nancie was carefully watching a ladybug on a nearby leaf.

"For example," said Mrs. Jordan, "*sensitivity to beauty* is one of your attributes, Nancie. You see beauty very clearly in the world around you.

"And the *love of learning* is one of your attributes, Krista. You love to discover new things."

With a grin, Krista said, "I think I'm doing that right now, Mrs. Jordan. I'm learning that since God is a *Person,* He has attributes too. Right?"

"Yes, indeed. But there's no label with a list of ingredients to tell us what they are.

"We learn of God's attributes as we read the Bible, just as we could discover *your* attributes, Nancie and Krista, if we read letters and poems and so on which you girls have written."

"So," said Nancie, "what will we discover in the Bible? What *are* God's attributes? What is He like?"

"Well," said Mrs. Jordan as she wrinkled her nose, "let me try to remember the names of these branches.

"Now that one over there, with the bird's nest on it—that's the Spirit Limb. *'God is spirit'*—Jesus Himself said that in John 4. God isn't wrapped up in a body like you and me. We get sick or tired or cold or hot, and all of us grow old. But none of that ever happens to God.

"There to your right is the Personal Limb. God is personal. Just like you and me, He knows things, He decides things, He does things, and He has feelings. He speaks to us, and we can speak to Him.

"Close to the Personal Limb is the Life Limb. God is life. But His kind of life is different from ours. We need food and air and warmth and rest and exercise to keep us alive, while God needs none of that. We can see this in the special name He has."

"You mean God has a name?" Krista asked.

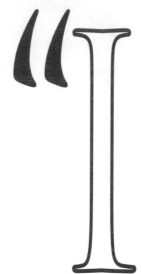

"Oh, what a name He has!" exclaimed Mrs. Jordan. "The Bible tells us that God's name is "<u>I AM</u>." Our Bibles often print the word <u>Lord</u> for this name. We can read in the book of Exodus of the time when God first told Moses His name. And now we can all use it when we talk to God in prayer.

"Just imagine, Nancie and Krista, what it would be like to live with someone the rest of your life, yet never know that person's name! God doesn't want it to be that way between us and Him, so He tells us what to call Him.

"It's a name we can count on! David says in Psalm 20, '*We <u>trust</u> in the name of I AM—the Lord our God.*'

"Yes, God is **I AM**; God is life. And that's why He can give life to others. As Paul reminds us in Acts 17, God gives all men '*life and breath and everything else.*' Just think: Every breath you take is a gift from God!"

Mrs. Jordan breathed out a loud puff of air, then the girls giggled and blew in each other's faces.

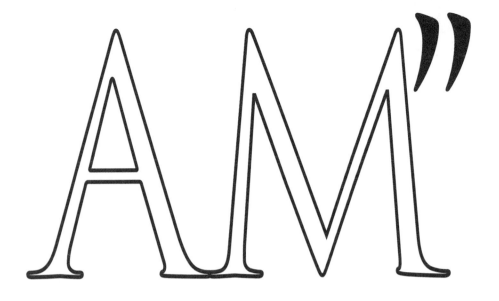

"Now, way over there," Mrs. Jordan continued, "is the Eternal Limb. God is eternal. Moses put it this way in his prayer in Psalm 90: *'From everlasting to everlasting, you are God.'* God has no beginning, and He has no end. And He's always the way He is. At this very moment, He's just as good and wise and great and loving as He was thousands of years ago when He spoke to Moses. In the book of Malachi, God says this: *'I the LORD do not change.'"*

"I suppose we could put it this way," said Nancie: "God is always as perfect…as He always is!"

Mrs. Jordan pointed up at another limb behind the girls. "I used to swing my legs over a branch that size, and hang upside down. Want to try it, Krista?" Krista nodded, and did.

While she was hanging, a quarter fell out of the pocket in her hiking shorts. Mrs. Jordan picked it off the ground and held it up.

"Now, isn't that interesting?" she said. "You're hanging from the Integrity Limb. God has integrity. That means He's totally fair and honest. We can trust Him. And this quarter here—just like all our coins and our dollar bills—is engraved with the words 'In God We Trust.' Not everyone who *spends* this money really trusts in God. But remember those words every time you hold a coin or dollar bill in your hands, and let it be a reminder that God truly can be trusted."

Mrs. Jordan threw the quarter up, and Krista caught it in her upside-down hands.

"By the way," Mrs. Jordan added, "let it also remind you to be fair and honest in how you *get* your money, and fair and honest in how you *spend* it. Never forget that it has God's name on it."

"This is wonderful," Nancie said, looking around the tree. "What else can we learn up here?"

"Well," said Mrs. Jordan, "I see the Everywhere Limb over there. God is everywhere. In the Bible He told the prophet Jeremiah that He was both *'a God nearby... and a God far away,'* and that He fills both heaven and earth. I can't be up in the tree and down here at the same time. But God can. He's up there with you, and He's down here with me, all at the same time. God is everywhere.

"That's why this hilltop is just as holy as a church. We can be just as near God here, or in a closet, or at school, or out in a corn-field, as we can anywhere else.

"No one can hide from God—though lots of sinful people want to. Because I see over there the Justice Limb. The Bible tells us that God is our Judge. All evil people who won't repent will be judged and punished for-ever, even though they may be rich and healthy and handsome here on earth. But those things don't matter to God. He has perfect justice."

"And the branch there with the kite stuck in it—that's the All-Knowing Limb, as I recall. God knows all there is to know. Psalm 147 says that His understanding has no limit— that He even knows each star by name. Jesus said that not even a little bird can fall to the ground without God knowing it, and that God knows how many hairs are on each of our heads. Scientists here on earth have made many discoveries, but God knew them all before the world was even made. He knows our every thought, even before we think them. Right now He knows everything that will ever happen in the future, plus everything that ever happened in the past. God even knows who that kite belongs to, and how it got stuck in the tree."

"Oh, I do too," said Nancie. "That's Ian's kite, and it got stuck up here one windy day last spring. I wish Ian and Jackson could be here to enjoy all that you're telling us, Mrs. Jordan. Please tell us more!"

"With pleasure," said Mrs. Jordan. "I especially remember that biggest limb across on the other side— it's the Holiness Limb. God is holy. That's not a big word, but it has a big meaning. One thing it means is simply that God is different from us. We're made in His image, but still we're not exactly like Him. Even in heaven, where we'll never sin again, we won't be God. We'll know Him better, but we'll still worship Him as our Lord and our Creator.

"The prophet Isaiah tells us how God is *'high and lifted up.'* He's as high above us as a night sky filled with stars, or a morning sky on fire with the sunrise.

"God's holiness also means that He can't even be touched by evil. That's why no man or woman or boy or girl who hasn't been made clean by the blood of Jesus Christ can enter God's heaven, where everything must be holy forever. God can't allow any evil in His presence. That's why even now He asks us to separate ourselves from what is unclean and sinful. Many times in the Bible God says, *'Be holy, for I am holy.'*

"Of course, you've already seen the Mercy Limb and the Love Limb. But let me tell you more about them."

"Close your eyes, girls," said Mrs. Jordan, "and soak up these things, just as those leaves soak up their nourishment from the branches and the trunk and the roots. It's what turns them green, you know.

"The Bible often matches the word *faithfulness* with the word *love*, to show us that God never lets up in His love. *Faithful* means never-failing. When God makes promises, we know He will keep them. He won't fail us. And He makes lots of promises in the Bible—as many as there are leaves on this tree!

He'll keep them, each and every one—because He is powerful, and He can do anything He wants to, and He *wants* to keep His promises to us. God is the greatest promise-maker there ever was; He's also the greatest promise-*keeper*, which is why *we* should keep our promises as well.

"Oh, and I can spot the Patience Limb, too. All through the Bible we see good men who made mistakes and failed God—Abraham, Moses, David, Peter, and others—but God never gave up on them.

"The Bible says also that the reason we haven't come yet to the end of time is that God is patient; He wants more people to give up their sins and be saved.

"God's loving care is all around. He's always giving, always sharing Himself. He isn't a stingy, scroogy God. No, He lavishes His love on us. His care is everywhere! He cares for this tree: He's the One who sends up that nourishment from the roots. He cares for the birds that nest in the branches, and the squirrels, and even that spider.

"And He's even more loving with you and me. None of us deserves such special care, but He gives it to us anyway. It's what we call God's grace—and here in the Tower Tree, the Grace Limb grows out of the Love Limb, just like the Mercy Limb does.

"Our salvation in heaven is God's gift to us, the gift of His grace. Paul tells us in his letter to the Ephesians, 'By grace you have been saved, through faith.'

"Sometimes we think of God's grace and mercy this way: His grace means giving us what we don't deserve: a home forever in heaven. And His mercy means not giving us what we do deserve—to be stuck in the prison of hell, far away from the light and love of God. No, God wants something better for us. He wants to see us become the perfect people He created us to be. His love and grace and mercy reach out to help us do just that."

"Are your eyes open now?" said Mrs. Jordan. "Just look at this sky! And those mountains! In Psalm 36, the Bible takes the biggest things we can see—the sky and the mountains and the ocean—and compares God's love and greatness to them, just to help us understand Him. Let me tell you about it."

"Psalm 36 is by David, and David says that God's faithful love reaches all the way to the sky, and His righteousness is like the mighty mountains. David also says that God's justice is as great as the ocean. All those vast, huge things reminded David of the vastness of God. They can do that for us as well.

"But actually, God's love is countless times bigger than the sky. His righteousness is countless times mightier than the most massive mountain. And His fairness is countless times deeper than the ocean.

"You know," said Mrs. Jordan, as she rested her hands on top of her head, "God is so vast, so huge, so complete and perfect, that He doesn't *need* anything or anybody. But that doesn't mean He's unfriendly. When He does something for us, it's because He truly loves us and wants to make us happy, and not because He needs something from us.

"That's why it's for our own good that He allows us to get to know Him. And it's to our own hurt if we don't take advantage of the opportunity!

"I'll even say this," Mrs. Jordan added, smiling up into the branches: "To have the chance to know God, and then not to take it, would be far worse than not climbing the Tower Tree whenever you could!"

Krista and Nancie thought silently for a long time. Nancie was thinking about God's greatness—all that He knows, and all that He can do and does do. Krista was thinking about His goodness— the tender way He treats us, and the never-failing love He shows us.

Then they both noticed a rustling noise nearby.

And there was Mrs. Jordan, climbing the Tower Tree until she reached the very top! She put her head up through the highest branches, and looked around. Krista and Nancie climbed up beside her.

"I'm sure you noticed," Mrs. Jordan said, "that all these branches are part of one tree. And all these attributes we've talked about—love, justice, holiness, patience, power, and so on—are part of One God. We can't say that one single branch shows us everything about this tree; in the same way, we can't say that just one or two of these attributes tells us everything about God. The tree is all of these branches, and God is all of those words, and many more besides.

"You know," she said, after taking in several big breaths of fresh air, "for us human beings, there'll always be lots of mystery about God, because there'll always be so much more to learn about Him. Why, even what we know already is more than we have the words to rightly express.

"There's no word good enough to tell how good He is. There's no word great enough to tell how great He is.

"But," she added, smiling at Nancie and Krista, "the words of the Bible are the perfect words for getting us going in the right direction! If you girls stay in your Bibles, you'll always be finding more reasons for having God as your Best Friend."

Gazing out from the treetop, Mrs. Jordan took one more look around in every direction.

> God is great, God is good; this He shows us in His Word!

SUPER TRUTH

Then her head suddenly dropped back into the leaves, and with a laugh she called out to Krista and Nancie:

"I'll race you to the ground!"

QUESTION CORNER

Whatever is true, whatever is noble, whatever is right, …<u>think about</u> such things.

Philippians 4:8

What is an attribute?

What does it mean that "God is spirit" (John 4:24)?

What is God's name? To whom did God first tell this name?

Why can we trust God? Should God trust US?

What does it mean that God is holy?

How does God show His love for us?

"NAILS DRIVEN IN FIRMLY"

The Word of God is not only like a hammer, but also like nails that the hammer drives in. In Ecclesiastes 12:11, the wise words of the Bible are said to be "like nails that have been driven in firmly. They are wise teachings that come from God the Shepherd."

Nails driven deep are not easy to pull out. Nails driven deep can turn a pile of boards into a treehouse, a packing crate or a front porch, then hold each one together for as long as it's needed. The more nails, the bigger and stronger can be the treehouse, the crate, or the porch.

Each nail is a wise teaching from God our Shepherd. How many nails—how many wise teachings from God—are driven deep into *your* life? Are the nails deep enough to stay? Are they deep enough to keep you from "falling apart" in tough times?

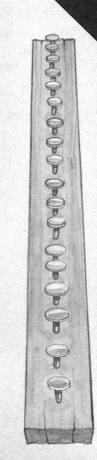

14 Three days later, on a rainy Saturday morning, Krista and Nancie joined Ian and Jackson at Skyler's house. Skyler's wife served them milk and cinnamon rolls, then they all pulled out their drawings to talk about them.

"So," began Skyler, "we've all been looking at Psalm 119—the longest chapter in the Bible. And by now you've probably discovered that it was written by someone who truly loved God's Word. But I won't say more until *you* do some talking first.

"Krista, what do you have there?"

Krista held up her drawing for everyone to see. "My favorite verses in Psalm 119," she explained, "are those which say that God's Words are sweet like honey (verse 103), and better than thousands of pieces of silver and gold (verse 72). God's Word is sweeter than honey...and better than money!"

"I like it!" said Jackson.

"Okay, Jackson, let's see yours."

"Here it is, folks," Jackson said. "That's me. I'm running a race...and I'm winning it, too!

"My favorite verse is number 32." Jackson opened his Bible and read the verse aloud: "*'I run in the path of your commands, for you have set my heart free.'* I'm sure that's a great feeling this guy had, just like I feel when I run faster than ever."

"Go for it, Jackson!" said Skyler. "And tell me: How do you think God's commands in the Bible can set a person free?"

"I think it's like this," answered Jackson: "When we learn in the Bible what God wants us to do, we know we can go right out and do it. We know He'll help us. He wouldn't ask us to do something if He wasn't going to help us do it.

"So whatever it is—helping someone, or not cheating, or not being mean, or whatever—we can do it without being afraid or worried. And we don't have to be slow about it. We can *run!*"

"Making Me Free to Run"

No One can tie up my mind

"Ian, you go next," said Nancie. "I got a look at yours already, and I think it's great."

"Thanks, Nancie. This is it." Ian held it up.

"Whoa!" Jackson exclaimed. "Who did he get mixed up with?"

"Somebody evil," Ian answered. "I drew this from verse 61: *'Though the wicked bind me with ropes, I will not forget your law.'* Skyler, you once told us that the worst thing an enemy could ever do was to keep us from thinking about God's Word. That's what I was reminded of when I saw this verse. Even if an enemy ties us up and throws us in prison, we'll still be free if we keep thinking about God's Word. No one can tie up our mind."

Then it was Nancie's turn.

"This is from verse 114," she said. "It's a prayer to God, and it goes like this: *'You are my refuge and my shield; I have put my hope in your word.'* In those days, a shield was a soldier's best protection. He wanted it wide and tall and thick. But in this psalm we learn that God and His Word give us even *better* protection. God and His Word can protect us from the worst enemy of all, Satan himself. Plus every other enemy as well."

The other children nodded in agreement. "I almost drew that verse too," Jackson said.

"So did I," said Ian.

"Well, I didn't," said Krista, "but it's a great verse to think about. I forget sometimes how much I need God's protection. I'm glad to know that the things I learn in the Bible will keep me safe."

"Okay, Captain Skyler," said Ian. "What do you have to show us?"

"A map of a dangerous place," answered Skyler, "I picked verse 19, which says this: *'I am a stranger on earth; do not hide your commands from me.'* I'm like you, Krista; too often I forget how much I need God—not only His protection, but also His guidance. I need Him to show me where to go and what to do.

"It helps me know how much I need God when I also remember that I'm just a stranger here on earth. Heaven is my real home, and until I go there to stay, I'm living on this alien planet with lots of dangers. God knows that, so He's given me a map to get me through it all. And that map is…"

"The Bible!" Jackson said.

"And it's a map with no mistakes!" Skyler added.

He and the children talked a little more, then put away their drawings. Then Krista asked, "When can we get together again and talk more about the Bible?"

Skyler looked over at his wife, who smiled and said, "You're all invited to a picnic here next Saturday—and bring your parents, too!"

Skyler leaned forward in his chair. "But before you leave today," he said, "let me give you something to take with you—a story about a great war…"

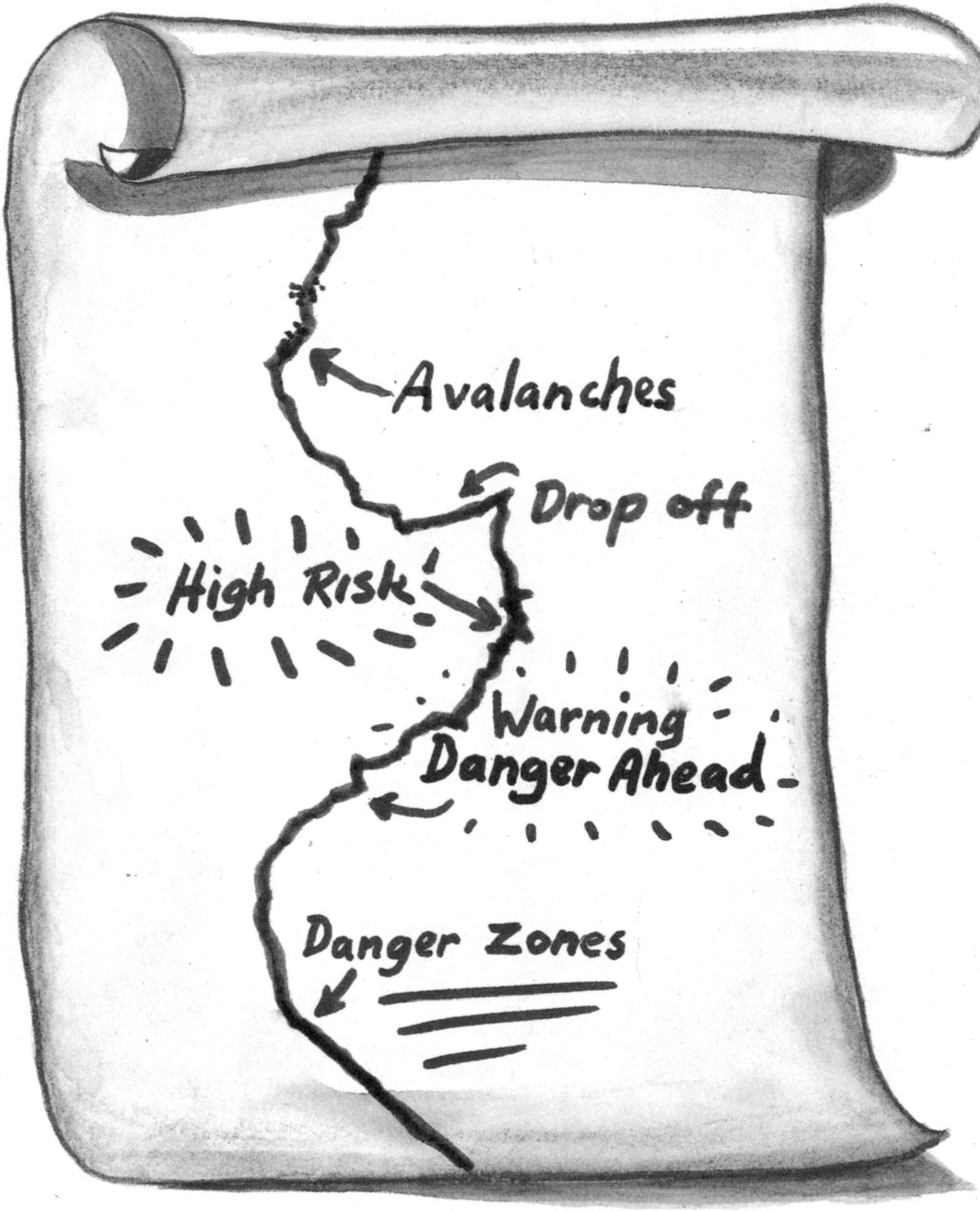

Avalanches
Drop off
High Risk
Warning
Danger Ahead
Danger Zones

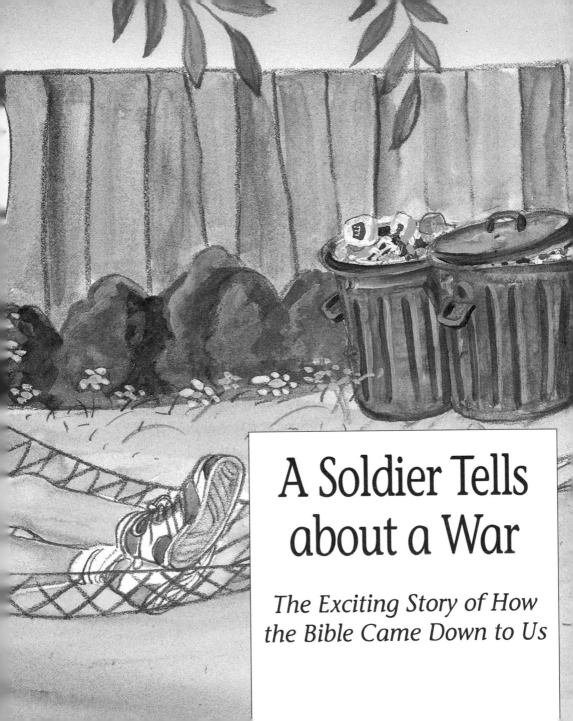

A Soldier Tells about a War

The Exciting Story of How the Bible Came Down to Us

15 The next afternoon—a quiet Sunday afternoon—Ian lay down in his backyard hammock, under a shady tree. He didn't mean to sleep. He just closed his eyes, and thought about the war story Skyler told them yesterday morning.

And then...Ian was face to face with a soldier! Not a modern soldier, but one from many centuries ago.

"Greetings, child of light," the soldier said.

Is he talking to me? Ian wondered.

The soldier turned, and began walking down a path. Ian found himself following close behind.

Still walking, the soldier turned his head to speak. "The battle has been fought since the beginning," he said. "It raged even in the land of Eden, in the Garden that was home for your forefather Adam, and Eve, his wife. For there the Satan-Snake began his deceitful temptation by disputing God's Word."

Ian stepped up to walk beside the soldier. But just then the soldier stopped and placed his hand on Ian's chest. "You can read about this," he said solemnly, "in your Bible. Read it…and take heed. For this is how the devil will also tempt you."

He resumed walking, and Ian quickly caught up.

"Always, always it is so," the soldier was saying. "The evil enemy does anything and everything to keep God's people from seeing and hearing and believing the Word of God for what it really is.

"He tries first to convince you that God's Words are only lies. If he cannot succeed in that, he will say God's Words are old-fashioned and foolish. If he doesn't win you there, he'll try to keep you so busy with other things that you don't have time for God's Words, no matter how highly you think of them.

"Satan's greatest joy would be for God's Words to be hidden away somewhere and forgotten forever."

The soldier lowered his voice. "It almost happened once, you know. In the time of King Josiah, workers came upon the scroll of the sacred Scriptures in the Temple, where it had long been hidden by the darkness and dust of God's forgetful people."

Suddenly the soldier stopped. "See it there!" he said. Ian looked where he pointed, and saw it.

"You yourself can read this in your Bible," the soldier said solemnly. "Read it, and take heed."

"Always, always a battle," the soldier said. He was walking again, faster this time. Ian hurried to his side, wondering where they were going.

"Some hear the Word of God," said the soldier, "but they despise what it says. For they know the Bible's power, and they know its truth. Yet in their wicked hearts they cannot accept it; they can only attack it. Pushed on by their father the devil, they fight the Scriptures, even with knife and fire.

"Yes, so it was, even with a king of Israel. In his own hands the king took the written Word of God as spoken through the prophet Jeremiah. He cut the sacred scroll to shreds, and threw the pieces in the fire at his side."

The soldier stopped again. "See it there!" he cried. Ian looked, and the sight made him shudder.

"You yourself can read this in your Bible," the soldier repeated solemnly. "Read it, child of light, and take heed. For whoever knows the truth and power of God's Word, and yet will not accept and obey it…in his hand also is the shredding knife. And at his side is the destroying fire."

"Always, always a battle," the soldier said. "And yet God Almighty is faithful, and keeps watch over His Word." The soldier looked into Ian's eyes and added, "For He knows there are some who will truly read it.

"Look there," the soldier said. Ian looked, and saw someone hiding scrolls in a cave.

"Those scrolls were hidden soon after Jesus lived on the earth," the soldier said. "The Romans were destroying Israel, so these Jews hid their copies of the Scriptures in caves beside the Dead Sea. All these Jews were killed. No one was left who knew about the scrolls.

"Two thousand years later, the enemies of God's Word were saying that today's Bible is not the same as the Bible in Jesus' day. They said that down through history, the people who wrote down new copies from the old scrolls probably made lots of mistakes in their writing. And since no one had any of the old scrolls anymore, they said there was no way to know if today's Bibles are correct.

"Then, not so many years ago, a little boy was herding goats near the Dead Sea. He tossed a rock into a cave, and he heard the sound of breaking pottery.

"He went to get a friend, and came back. They went down in the cave and found pottery jars filled with the ancient Scripture scrolls. Later, in other caves nearby, more Scripture scrolls were found.

"These old scrolls proved that today's Scriptures are just like the ones Jesus read and taught. Today's Bibles are just as trustworthy as ever.

"You can be sure," the soldier said, looking again into Ian's eyes, "that today's Bible is God's Word."

"Always, always a battle," said the soldier, as he continued walking. "And especially fierce was the fight to get the Bible into English.

"Today, English is the world's most important language; therefore the Bible in English is the world's most important book. That's why, hundreds of years ago, when English was spoken by only a few million people on the little island of England, Satan did all he could to keep those people from having a Bible in English. Many leaders in England were the very worst about carrying out Satan's plans.

"A man named John Wycliffe wrote down the first Bible in English. But the leaders were angry about this. After he died, the leaders dug up John Wycliffe's bones and threw them into a river.

"Look there," said the soldier. "What do you see?"

"Oh!" Ian cried in horror. He saw a man being burned alive!

"That man is William Tyndale," the soldier said. "He also wrote down the Bible in English, and had it printed in books so people everywhere in England could read it.

"But the king of England and other leaders hated him for it. First they put him in prison. Then they brought him here, to burn him at the stake.

"Now listen," said the soldier. "What do you hear?"

Ian listened. William Tyndale was saying something: "Lord," he cried with his last breath, "open the king of England's eyes!" Then he dropped his head. He died as the flames rose higher.

"God answered that dying prayer," the soldier said. "Seventy years later, a new king of England—King James— brought together many Bible teachers and wise men and writers. Together they wrote down the most powerful book the world has ever known: the great King James Version of the Bible. This was the Bible that went every- where in the world as English became a world language."

The soldier kept marching onward. Ian was getting tired, and was having trouble keeping up.

The soldier looked back, then stopped and said, "Here's a resting place."

They sat down on some stones.

"Child of light," said the soldier, "the Bible is a great and wonderful book. Do you know why?"

"It's great and wonderful," Ian said, "because it's God's Book, and God is great and wonderful."

"True and well spoken," said the soldier. "And do you know a second reason?"

Ian thought for a moment. "Surely the Bible is also great and wonderful…because it tells us great and wonderful things. It tells us about Jesus!"

"Again, a wise answer," said the soldier. "Can you give a third reason?"

"It's great and wonderful…because it's written in a great and wonderful way—full of beauty and power!"

The soldier smiled. Ian was glad his answers were pleasing.

"There is yet a fourth reason," said the soldier, without losing his smile. "Do you now know it?"

Ian felt the right words coming into his heart and mind, and onto his lips: "I believe I do, sir. The Bible is a great and wonderful book, because it has come to us in a great and wonderful way—through a great war with the evil one."

The soldier was solemn again. "You have answered truly, child of light. And now know this: The battle rages still, and *you* are a soldier in this war."

They rose, walked on, then stopped once again.

"Look and see," the soldier said to Ian. "This woman is learning a language that does not yet have a written Bible. When she learns this language, she will write down the Bible in these new words. Then the people who speak this language can learn all about Jesus.

"At this very moment, she is doing this. She, too, is a soldier in the war today. And there are thousands like her."

They kept walking along the path. The soldier was silent now. At his side, Ian was quiet also. But he had so many questions in his head: *Where does this path lead? Who is this soldier? What is his name, and where did he come from? Why am I going with him?*

Soon Ian saw a light ahead, a warm light that was growing and filling his vision. He remembered all the things the soldier had shown him—the temptation of Adam and Eve, the scroll being found in the Temple, the king cutting and burning Jeremiah's words, the Dead Sea scrolls, Wycliffe and Tyndale and the King James Bible, and the modern missionaries translating the Bible into new languages. Now he remembered that all of this had been part of the story Skyler Brown gave them yesterday morning. *Skyler had told them everything.*

The warm light grew brighter. Ian couldn't see the soldier anymore. He blinked his eyes.

Then he looked up into blinding light. He saw the sun just below the shade-line of the trees, and it was shining full on his face. Ian woke up.

He rose from the hammock. Then he walked inside to get his Bible…on this quiet Sunday afternoon.

QUESTION ■CORNER

Why is the Bible a great and wonderful Book?

What do YOU see in these verses in Psalm 119: 19, 32, 61, 72, 103, 114, 127.

What do YOU see? Read about the scroll found in the Temple in 2 Chron. 34:14-33.

What do YOU see? Read about the king burning Jeremiah's scroll in Jeremiah 36.

Who was John Wycliffe? Who was William Tyndale?

Why are the "Dead Sea Scrolls" important?

MAKING US CLEAN

On their last night together before Jesus was put to death on the cross, He told His disciples that He had made them *clean* by the words He had spoken to them.

For three years these men had been following Jesus, and they heard Him say many things. From these words they had learned so much about their sin, about obeying God, and about living a life of love. That's what becoming clean was all about!

God's Word make *us* clean as well. Many times we don't *feel* loving and good; our minds are far from God. But if we realize this, and then open our Bibles and let His Words rinse over us, we'll feel the dirt washing away. Our souls need a shower as often as our bodies do!

Go ahead and try it...the next time you feel mean or crabby or worried. Let God's Word make you happy and clean!

A Flavorful Feast

The Bible as Our Spiritual Food...and More!

16

"Good food, hey guys?" Skyler asked.

The children had their mouths full, but they all nodded. Ian and Nancie were enjoying fried chicken. Jackson had finished two hot dogs, and now was eating green peas. So was Krista.

"They're my favorite vegetable," Krista said.

"Probably mine too," said Jackson, as he sprinkled salt and pepper on his.

"Yuck," said Ian. "How can you guys stand those things?"

"Because they belong to God," Jackson answered, "but He gave them to us."

"That's true of everything we eat," Nancie said.

"Yeah, but it's especially true of peas," replied Jackson. "It's even in the Bible." He opened his mouth and ate a big spoonful of them.

Ian thought about what Jackson said. "What do you mean?" he finally asked.

A twinkle appeared in Jackson's eye. "Oh, you know," he said. "We had the verse last week in Sunday school: the one in John 14 where Jesus says, 'Peas I leave with you; my peas I give to you.'"

"Oh, but that's *peace,* not *peas,*" protested Nancie. Then she and Ian noticed Jackson's grin. "Ohhh," said Nancie with a shrug and a laugh, "he's teasing again!"

"Well, anyway," Jackson said, "eating peas makes me peaceful."

Ian only groaned.

Skyler was sitting with their parents, telling them how fun it was to study the Bible with their children.

Everyone had berries and shortcake and whipped cream for dessert. Then Skyler asked the grown-ups if they would share a few words with the whole group about what the Bible means to them.

Krista's mother spoke first. "I've been a bread-baker for years," she said with a smile, "and how I love the smell of it, fresh from the oven!

"One of my favorite verses is the one that says, *'Man does not live on bread alone, but on every word that comes from the mouth of God.'* I know God's Word is as satisfying and nourishing—and as *flavorful*—as every bite of that fresh hot bread."

"I'm a fireman," said Jackson's father, "and I see again and again how awesome a fire can be. That's why I like Jeremiah 23:29, where God says His Word is like fire. I like to think of all the *energy* that's in the Bible, with the power to burn away bad things in our lives, and to fire us up to do good things.

"I also want to say how proud I am of Jackson, and all you children, for getting such a good start on understanding the Scriptures."

"Same here," said Ian's father. "And I also like that verse in Jeremiah 23, because it goes on to say that God's Word is like a hammer. I'm a carpenter, and I use a hammer every day. A hammer has power, too—power to break, and power to build. I know it's the same with the Bible: God's Word can break down the hardness of heart we sometimes have, and it can also build us up, and make us new and right inside!"

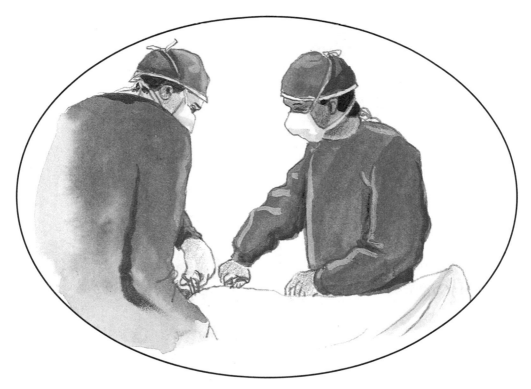

"My favorite verse," said Nancie's father, "is the one in Hebrews 4 that says the Word of God is sharper than a two-edged sword. It says that God's Word *'cuts all the way into us, where the soul and the spirit are joined. It cuts to the center of our joints and our bones.'*

"I'm a surgeon. So I understand why God uses His Word to cut so deep inside us: He wants to heal us in our hearts, and He wants to keep us well inside."

Skyler's wife spoke next: "I've been thinking about a passage in the book of James that compares the Word of God to a mirror.

"It's amazing the way you can be reading in the Bible, and suddenly you see so clearly something in your life that you need to change …or it might be something else that God is pleased about and wants you to keep doing. Without the Bible, you can't really know who you are, just as you can't know what you really look like without a mirror."

The grown-ups were silent now, and so were the children. Skyler took a look at their thoughtful faces.

"What's on your mind?" he asked them.

Nancie crossed her arms, and said, "I didn't realize the Bible could do so much. Although I guess it's really God who does it…and the Bible is His way of telling us what He needs to tell us to get the job done!"

"Skyler," said Ian, "I hope you'll keep studying the Bible with us kids, even though summer will soon be over, and we'll be busy with school-work."

"Oh, yes," said Krista. "Please give us a Bible study assignment, Skyler, like what we did with Psalm 119."

"Yeah, and let's draw something again," Jackson said. "I'm a good artist, as well as a good runner."

"Okay," laughed Skyler. "I just thought of something fun. Tell me, Jackson: What did you put on your peas when you ate them today?"

"Pepper and salt," he answered.

"Why?"

"Because I like them salty and peppery. They taste better that way. More flavor, more fun!"

"Good answers," said Skyler. "And here's another question, for all of you: When you see a movie or read a story, and you really like it—what makes you like it?"

"A good hero, and lots of action!" said Ian. "Like a narrow escape, or a big fight."

"Or something scary," agreed Jackson.

"Not for me," said Nancie. "I want lots of feelings, lots of emotion. Like a broken heart, or becoming best friends, or living happily ever after."

"Great answers," said Skyler. "You know, I'd say *action* and *emotion* are the salt and pepper of any good book—the things that make a story fun and fulfilling to read. And it just so happens that God's Book has lots of action and emotion in it, too. It's our spiritual food—and it's full of flavor!

> **SUPER TRUTH**
>
> The Bible, our spiritual food, is full of flavor!

"I'd like each of you to choose your own passage of Scripture to read and study. And when we get back together next week, show me a drawing of the action or the emotion—or both—which you find in that passage. How does that sound?"

"Salt and pepper," said Jackson. "Sounds like fun!"

"Let's do it!" said Krista.

17 "Wow," said Jackson. "Who's that?"

Skyler and the children were sitting on a long wooden bench inside a shopping mall. A fountain splashed beside them. They were taking their first look at Nancie's drawing of action or emotion.

"Can you guess who they are?" asked Nancie.

None of the children could.

"Are you sure this is in the Bible?" said Ian.

Skyler spoke up: "I'm sure it is. And I'll make a guess: I think it's Job and his wife, from the book of Job."

Nancie smiled. "You're right, Skyler. I found lots of emotion—and lots of action, too—when I got into that book. Satan killed all of Job's children, and all of his servants, and all of his farm animals. Then he covered Job's entire body with painful sores."

"Ugh," Jackson said, rubbing his arms.

"And now," continued Nancie, "Job's wife tells him he ought to curse God and die. But Job never does that, as far as I can tell. I skipped over to the end of the book, and it looks like Job lived happily ever after—just the kind of ending I like."

"Thank you, Nancie," said Skyler. "Splendid work. Okay, Ian: You're on."

Ian brought out his drawing. "I decided to read Paul's two letters to Timothy. He wrote the second letter while he was in prison. In chapter four, it looks like Paul will soon be killed, and he knows it.

"But he isn't sad. This is what he says:

> "'The time has come for me to leave this life. I have fought the GOOD FIGHT. I have finished the race. I have kept the faith. Now, a crown is waiting for me. I will get that crown for being right with God. The Lord is the judge who judges rightly, and he will give me the crown on that Day. He will give that crown not only to me but to all those who have waited with love for Jesus to come again.'"

Ian seemed to have a tear in his eye as he said, "For the first time I understand that Paul was a hero— a *great* hero."

"Oh, that's *beautiful*," said Nancie.

Krista was next. "I read the book of Esther," she began. "It has lots of action and lots of emotion too. Esther was a beautiful woman, and the King of Persia chose her to be his queen. He didn't know she was a Jew —one of God's people.

"There was a wicked man who was the king's assistant. This man tricked the king into giving an order to kill every Jew in Persia.

"Esther had a cousin, an old man named Mordecai. Mordecai pleaded with Esther to go to the king and to beg him not to kill all the Jews.

"But in those days, you couldn't just go and talk to the king, unless he first asked you to. The punishment was death for anyone who came into his presence without first being invited. Esther knew she might be put to death if she went to ask for the king's mercy.

"But Esther was as brave as she was beautiful. She made up her mind to go talk to the king. And she said, 'If I die, I die.' That's what my drawing is all about."

"So what happened next?" asked Jackson.

"You should read it for yourself," answered Krista. "You'll enjoy it more that way."

"Ohhhh," Jackson groaned.

"Let's see yours, Jackson," Ian said.

"I wanted to read all about David," Jackson said, "and how he became king in place of King Saul, after Saul tried to kill him. I started in 1 Samuel, and I found lots of neat action to draw. But I was enjoying the story so much that I just kept reading.

"Then I came to the part where King Saul finally died in a battle that the Philistines won against Israel. That was at the very end of 1 Samuel. I was glad to find the story continued in 2 Samuel, and I kept reading. The man who was trying to kill David— because he didn't want him to be king—was finally dead himself, and I wanted to know how David would react when he found out about it.

"David surprised me. I can hardly believe how hard he took the news. Saul's son Jonathan was killed too, and Jonathan was David's best friend; so I can understand David being upset over Jonathan. But he seemed even more upset about Saul. He wrote a really sad song about it.

"So that's what I drew. And I ended up with a picture about feelings instead of a picture of action."

"Well," said Skyler, "I also decided on a picture of emotion instead of action. I've been studying the little books of First, Second and Third John—John's three letters.

"I drew it just this morning, after I was struck by something I read in the third letter. John was writing to a man named Gaius. John had just been told by someone that Gaius was faithfully following the way of truth. Gaius was living the kind of life that proved how much he loved Jesus.

"As John began his letter, he told Gaius what he had heard about him. Then he added, *'I have no greater joy than to hear that my children are walking in the truth.'*

"Gaius was not really one of John's children. But John had taught Gaius about Jesus, perhaps many years earlier. Gaius never forgot. Now John felt happy for him, like a proud father does.

"You know," said Skyler, "I feel the same way about you four kids. And I pray I always will. Ten and twenty and thirty years from now, when perhaps we're all living many miles apart, I hope I get letters telling me how much all of you still love and obey the God of the Bible."

QUESTION CORNER

Whatever is true,
whatever is noble,
whatever is right,
...think about
such things.

*Philippians
4:8*

How is the Bible like a mirror?

How is the Bible like bread? Like fire? Like a hammer? Like a sword?

See for yourself: Read about God's Word in Matt. 4:4, Jer. 23:29, and Heb. 4:12.

What action and emotion do you see in your favorite stories and teachings of the Bible?

Which men and women in the Bible do you think of as heroes?

What do YOU like to see in a movie or book?

"SOLID FOOD"

DISCOVER
Hebrews
5:12-14

Do you want your body to grow up? If so, you've probably got an appetite that proves it! To build a tall and strong body, good solid food is a must.

In Hebrews 5 we read about "solid food" that helps Christians grow spiritually. This food is a richer kind of Bible teaching that goes beyond the ABC's for beginners. It's for believers who are growing wise and mature in how they live for Jesus, and who can easily tell the difference between right and wrong.

You may be a beginner in your Christian life—and that's okay. Everyone has to make a start! Do your best to make it a *good* start, so you can grow up just as much spiritually as you will physically.

As you do, you'll find new solid food in God's Word, food that tastes better than any you've ever had!

Playground Promises

*How the Bible Helps Us
in Everyday Life*

18 Summer vacation came to an end...and so did the first day of school. After classes, Krista, Nancie, Ian, and Jackson joined several other children for some fun on the playground. Skyler was planning to meet them there soon.

For Ian and Jackson, the fun quickly turned into a fight. Nancie and Krista watched in dismay.

The fight was over and the dust had settled when Skyler approached. From the looks of Ian and Jackson, he could tell he had come on the heels of a scuffle.

"Well," he said, looking over the two boys. "Were you fighting each other?"

"No sir," Ian responded. "We were mostly fighting Reggie Longman. A few others joined in."

"Hmm," said Skyler. "I hear Reggie Longman is about the toughest kid in school."

"Well *he* sure thinks so," said Jackson.

"So who threw the first punch?"

"The first one wasn't a punch," admitted Jackson. "Reggie was walking away, and I tripped him."

"Why did you trip him?"

"Well," Jackson began with a sigh, "we told everybody today what we've been learning this summer about the Bible. Lots of kids thought it was great. But after school, Reggie came up and said the Bible is nothing but a bunch of fairy tales that aren't true, and only a half-brain would believe anything in it. And he strutted away like he thought we were too stupid to know any better."

Skyler looked sad. "That's why you tripped him?"

Jackson paused. "Well, not exactly. As he was walking away, he said one more thing."

"Which was?"

"Well..." Jackson slowly scratched his forehead.

"Go on," said Skyler.

"He said, 'Everybody knows a Four-Eyes has only half a brain anyway.'" Now that Jackson repeated it, he knew it was nothing to start a fight over.

Skyler looked even sadder. He turned to Ian. "And you? Why did you jump in on this?"

"To be honest," Ian said, "I've been mad at Reggie all day. He laughed his head off this morning when I told my class that I got sick on the helicopter." Then Ian shrugged, and added, "I'm glad I bloodied his nose."

Now Skyler really looked disappointed. But then he halfway smiled, rubbed his hand in Ian's ruffled hair, and clapped his other hand on Jackson's shoulder. "Let's all have a talk," he said.

"Us too?" said Nancie.

"Why not?" Skyler said, with a real smile at the girls.

They sat down on a patch of grass.

"I had something else ready to share with you," Skyler said, "but I suppose I'll save it for later."

He sat and thought for a moment. The children were just as silent as he was.

He turned to the boys, and said quietly, "If you guys had your Bibles with you, and if I had a pair of scissors in my pocket, do you know what I might do just now?"

Scissors? they wondered. "No sir," said Ian. "What?"

"I'd take out my scissors," Skyler continued softly, "and ask you for your Bibles. Then I'd cut out lots and lots of verses from them. Like Proverbs 29:11—'*A fool gives full vent to his anger, but a wise man keeps himself under control.*' Or Proverbs 25:28—'*Like a city whose walls are broken down is a person who has no self-control.*'

"And of course, I'd have to cut out Jesus' words in Matthew 5, where He tells us not to fight back against someone who is bad to us, but to even offer our other cheek when someone slaps us. And 1 Peter 3:9 would have to be cut out. That's the one that says, '*Do not repay evil with evil or insult with insult, but with blessing.*'"

Jackson suddenly felt like crying. Ian still felt angry, but he wasn't sure who he was angry at. *Was it himself?*

Skyler folded his arms on his chest. "No," he said, "I really wouldn't cut out those verses from your Bibles. It would make no difference anyway. God's Words don't go away just because we forget them, or ignore them."

"I'm sorry, Skyler," said Jackson.

Ian thought more about it. He knew he'd been wrong. But was it God he was angry at?

"I'm sorry, too," Ian said.

"For what?" Skyler asked.

"For losing my temper with Reggie," Ian answered.
Jackson nodded. "Yeah, me too."

"So who do you need to apologize to?" Skyler said.

"Reggie," answered Ian. Jackson nodded again.

"Anyone else?" Skyler asked.

"And God," Ian said after a moment. *"But Skyler,"* he
burst out, "it's so awful hard to do everything God tells
us to! He tells us so much, and it's just so *hard!*"

"I know how you feel," Skyler answered calmly. "By the way, if I cut up *your* Bible to get rid of all the verses you've disobeyed, I'd have to cut out even more from *mine.* Because I'm a sinner too. I've broken a ton of God's commands in my lifetime.

"But really, I didn't sin because of how hard God's commands are, but because of how hard *I* am.

"Let me read to you one of my favorite Scripture passages. It's from 1 John 5."

Skyler opened his Bible, and read aloud:

"Loving God means obeying his commands. And God's commands are <u>not too hard for us</u>. Everyone who is a child of God has the power to win against the world."

SUPER TRUTH

God's commands are not too hard for us!

Skyler closed his Bible. "So," he said, "God's children really do have the power to obey God's commands and to win against all the bad things in the world. But when I think of that passage, I like to match it with a verse in 1 John 3." Skyler quoted it from memory: *"How great is the love the Father has lavished on us, that we should be called children of God! And that is what we are!"*

Skyler put his arms around the boys. "God loves us, Ian! He loves us, Jackson! *That's* why we're His children.

"God proved His love when He sent Jesus to suffer and die for us. So now we have a choice. We have two ways to view God's commandments. We can think of them as a 60-pound backpack that we have to carry for the rest of our lives. Or we can trust in God's love, and think of His commands as a bright, cool T-shirt we get to wear, with the words *I AM LOVED* across the front of it."

"Somedays, when you really think about that love, it's as if beautiful fireworks are exploding in your heart. You're fired up to do anything God tells you to.

"On other days you won't feel the same excitement, but that's okay. Our faith doesn't depend on our feelings, anyway. We know He loves us; so we pray and tell Him we trust Him. Then we go ahead and do what He tells us to in His Bible, because we know He'll give us the strength to do it.

"And if we make mistakes, if we stumble and fall, we simply tell God about it as soon as possible. We confess our sin, and we receive His forgiveness. Then we get back up and enjoy life in our beautiful T-shirt."

Ian smiled, and exchanged a look with Jackson.

"I think we're both ready to pray," Jackson said. "Then we'll go find Reggie and apologize.

"And then," he added, "will you tell us how to answer someone who says the Bible's only fairy tales?"

19

"Fairy tales, huh?" said Skyler.

Ian and Jackson had just returned from apologizing to Reggie and his friends. Jackson said it went fine. But just as he and Ian had turned to leave, Reggie called out, "By the way, Four-Eyes, I still think the Bible is a bunch of fairy tales!"

"And how did you respond this time?" said Skyler.

"I hurried back here to get your answer to my earlier question," said Jackson. "I was even wondering if it really makes any difference whether the Bible is true or not."

"What do you think?"

"It probably does," said Jackson, "but I'd like to know exactly why."

"I'd like to know too," Krista said. Ian and Nancie agreed.

"I believe I have a good reason for you," Skyler said. "It comes down to this: Who is now your Lord and Master?"

"Jesus is," Nancie answered.

"Then the right question to ask is this: *What does Jesus think of the Bible? Right?*"

"That makes sense," said Jackson. "So what *does* Jesus think of it?"

"You could put every verse in the Gospels under a microscope," Skyler said, "without finding a single place where Jesus shows the Scriptures to be anything but true. And not only true, but also as a *final authority,* as the very Word of God. On one occasion He said this: *'Scripture cannot be broken.'*

"So that's our starting place: Jesus Christ teaches us that the Bible is true, and the Bible is our authority from God."

"Some people use the word *inerrant* to describe the Scriptures. When you say something is *inerrant,* that word simply means that it 'doesn't wander away.'

"So," Skyler said, "what picture comes to your mind when you think of wandering away?"

"Let's see," Nancie answered. "I think of a jittery rabbit who hops off the trail and hides away in some briar bushes."

"Good image," Skyler said. "The Bible never wanders like that. The Bible stays on the path of truth. The Bible's teachings stay clear and clean."

The Bible never wanders from the truth.

SUPER TRUTH

"And I'm glad it stays clean and clear, because it's our authority. What do you think of when you hear the word *authority?*"

Ian answered first: "I think of the police."

"You're right, Ian. The police have authority over us. If I'm driving too fast, the police can stop me and make me pay a fine. If I steal something, the police can catch me and take me to jail. The police are a part of our government, and they have the authority to do those things.

"The reason they have that authority is that God gives it to them in the Bible. He tells us in Romans 13 to obey government authorities, and that the only authority these people have is what God has given them.

"But God doesn't pass along to the police or any-one else in government the authority to tell us how we should think, or what we should believe about Jesus Christ, or how to find happiness in our hearts, or how to be truly wise and truly loving. We go straight to God's Word to find those answers, because only God has authority in those areas. And He tells us everything we need to know in the Bible."

"I have a question," Krista said. "If the Bible is made up of God's Words, why did He use human beings like Moses and Paul to write it?"

"I don't know for sure," Skyler answered. "God can do anything He wants to, so He really doesn't *have* to use people to do anything. Yet He *does* use people in His work, again and again.

"It just seems to be part of His love for us. I'm sure He loved men like Moses and Paul and John and David very much, and part of His love for them was to let them write His Bible—just as your parents often let you help them bake a cake or fix the car or paint the house.

"And what a privilege it was for Moses and John and the others to be given a part in writing down words that will last forever!"

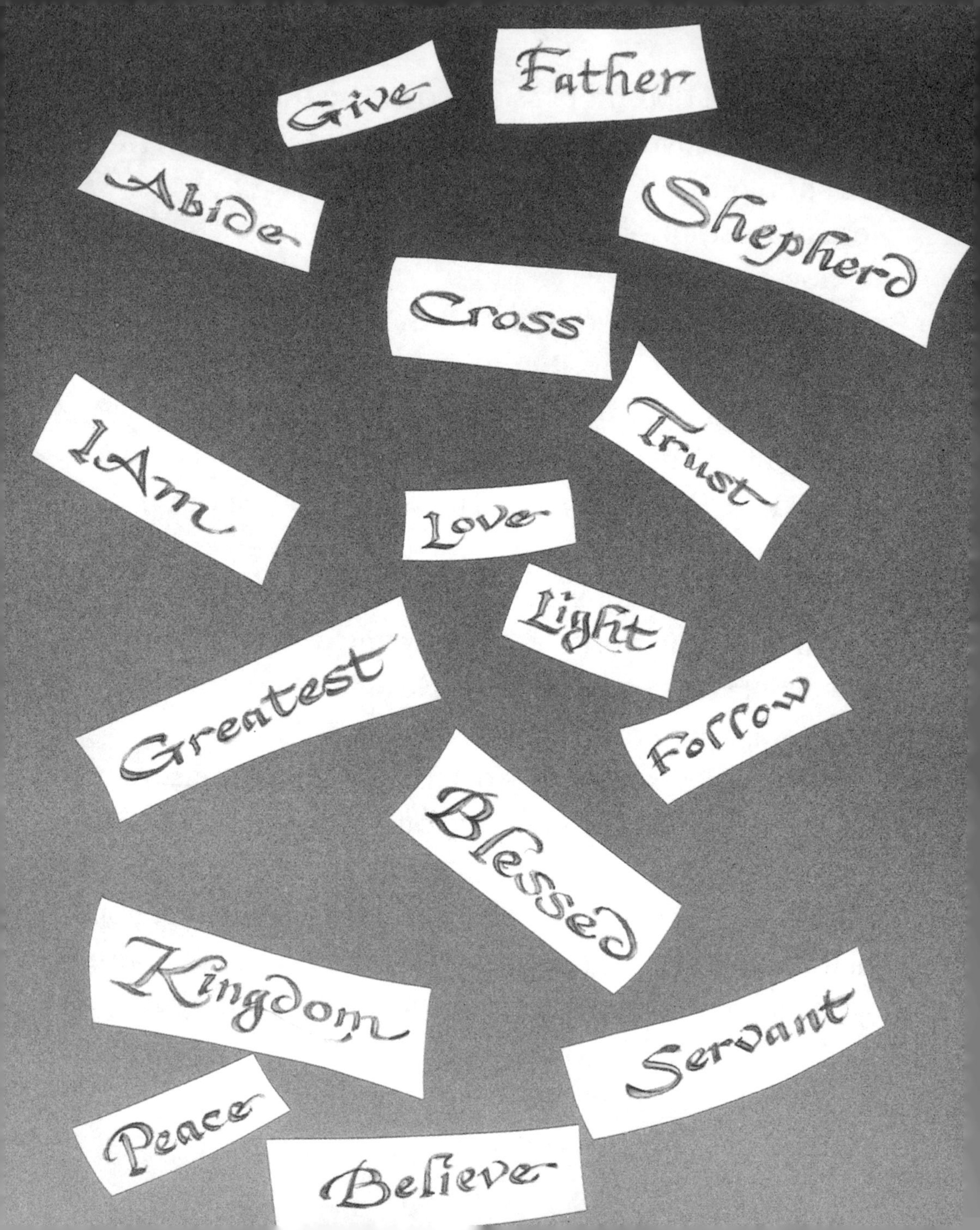

Give

Father

Abide

Shepherd

Cross

Trust

I Am

Love

Light

Greatest

Follow

Blessed

Kingdom

Servant

Peace

Believe

"Jesus once said this: *'The sky and the earth will pass away, but My Words will never pass away.'* His Words have more staying power than even the ground we're walking on, or the sky above us. We can't say that about your words or my words or Reggie Longman's words; but about God's Words we can. When *He* says something, it rings out forever."

"Skyler, I have a question too," Jackson said. "Why does someone like Reggie Longman say that the Bible is only a fairy tale?"

"Why do *you* think he says that, Jackson?"

"You know, Skyler, I just think he doesn't understand."

"Understand *what?*"

Jackson thought for a moment, then carefully spoke his answer: "That God really does love him, and wants Reggie to live with Him in heaven, and has given him a Book to tell him all about it."

Skyler nodded. "Now, to help Reggie learn those things," he said, "it's a good thing we've decided to stop fighting him and start loving him, right?"

"Right," Jackson said with a smile.

QUESTION ■CORNER

■ Whatever is true,
whatever is noble,
whatever is right,
...<u>think about</u>
such things.

*Philippians
4:8*

What does Jesus Christ think of the Bible?

Is the Bible more like a heavy backpack to you, or a cool T-shirt?

Are there any verses that people who know you might want to cut out of YOUR Bible?

What's good to do when we don't feel excited about God's commands in the Bible?

What's good to do when we know we have disobeyed God's Word?

What does it mean that the Bible is "inerrant"?

"PURE MILK"

Have you noticed how hungry babies go after their milk? God gives them a built-in craving for it. Peter had this in mind when he wrote his first letter in our Bibles. He tells us to desire the pure Word of God with the same craving healthy babies have for their milk.

God's Word is pure and wholesome and nourishing. There are many other things we sometimes have a craving for which are *not* pure and wholesome and nourishing. In fact, those things can stop our spiritual growth. As the saying goes, "Some people never grow up!"

Unless they're sick, babies don't need to be persuaded to take their milk. But sometimes we need a reminder to take our spiritual milk. David says in Psalm 34:8, "Taste and see that the Lord is good." Keep tasting the Scriptures —drink them up!—and find out how good our God is.

Encounter in the Heavens

*How Christ Is There
in All the Scriptures*

20 It was mostly Krista's, Ian's, Nancie's, and Jackson's idea. Skyler loved the plan, and he quickly added a lot to it.

The children wanted a fun way to tell their friends more about the Bible, as Skyler had done for them. Skyler said he couldn't take all their friends on a helicopter ride, so they decided on a different kind of trip: an imaginary space journey through the solar system. Each planet would represent one of the parts of the Bible—Torah, History, Prophets, and so on.

"What do we do with the sun?" Krista asked.

"Ah, I know exactly what to do with it," Skyler said. He told them, and they agreed it was perfect.

Saturday afternoon came, the day of the big spaceship show. Kids from the neighborhood started arriving more than an hour early. When Nancie's back yard was almost full of kids and cats and dogs, Skyler began.

"Ladies and gentlemen and animals," he said with a smile, "fasten your seatbelts for a space trip that will be truly an encounter in the heavens…"

"This incredible voyage," said Skyler, "is a journey like no other you've ever taken or even attempted. This is a trip not only to delight your eyes and challenge your mind, but also to thrill your soul. For you see, on this great adventure we'll be encountering the Creator and Lord of the universe. And we'll follow His Cosmic Code-Book as our guide to all the mysteries of the universe."

Inside an old refrigerator container box nearby, Krista whispered to Nancie, Ian, and Jackson: "Skyler's good at this, isn't he?"

They all nodded.

"Now," Skyler went on, "we'll launch our journey right from the surface of the sun. *But, you may ask, how can we withstand the terrible heat there?* Ah, the answer is simple. Won't you please look behind you!"

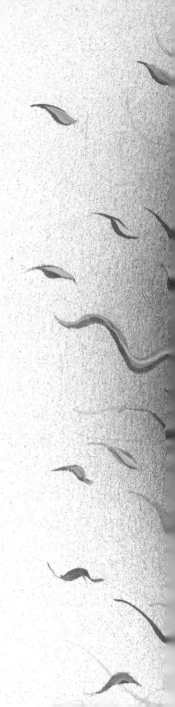

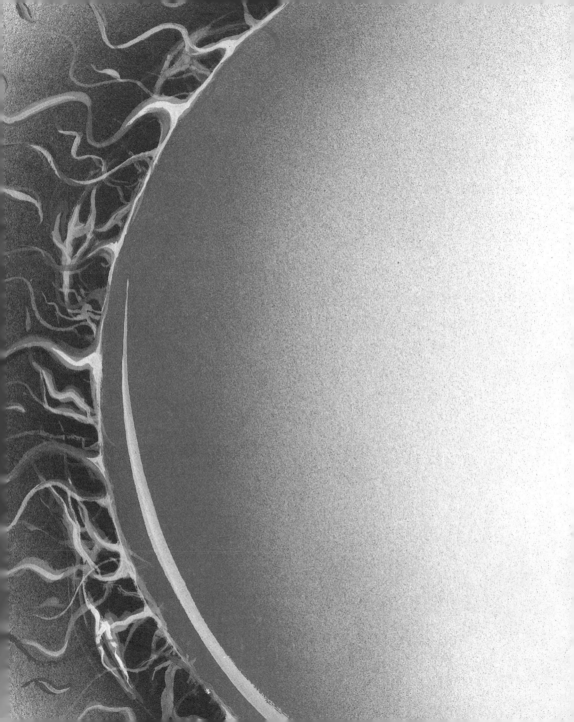

"Yes, ladies and gentlemen, that's fresh, cool lemonade! You'll find extra cups under the table, and we can also bring out more lemonade from inside. Help yourself at any time during the trip.

"And there's another reason we won't get roasted near the sun. Our amazing spaceship is very well insulated. Even though we'll be moving right through the sun's fingers of flame, you'll feel no warmer than you would if you were, say, 93 million miles away, on a pleasant late summer's day.

"*And why,* you may wonder, *are we taking off from the sun?* Ah, the answer is simple.

"As you know, the sun is the very center of the solar system. The sun is what holds our solar system together.

"But there's a *Person* who holds the entire universe together, and He holds all of life together, too. He holds you together and me together. He holds atoms and molecules together. He can hold families together. He can hold our minds and hearts together. In fact, our Cosmic Code-Book says this about the amazing Person I'm speaking of: '*In Him ALL THINGS hold together.*'

"*And what,* you may ask, *is this Cosmic Code-Book?* Ah, the answer is simple. It's the Bible, the Most Amazing Book in All the Universe!

"*And who,* you may ask, *is this Person who holds everything together?* Ah, the answer is simple: His name is Jesus, and from the Bible we'll help you see just how wonderful He really is. *HE* is what this tremendous trip is all about.

"Now, as you may have noticed, our well-insulated spaceship has a window. It looks sort of like a hole cut in the side of a box that once held a refrigerator. But actually, it's our window to the stars.

"And through that window, YOU'LL SEE EACH PLANET AS WE APPROACH IT..."

Skyler said the last sentence very loudly, because that was the cue for the children inside the refrigerator box to hold up their first poster in the window. It was a beautiful picture of the planet Mercury.

"Why, look there!" said Skyler, pointing to the poster in the box-window. "I believe we're already coming near our first planet.

"Yes, it's Mercury, the planet that's closest to the sun. By the way—as you may know, the planet Mercury has no light of its own. The only reason we can see it, is that it reflects the light of the sun.

"In the same way, the first part of the Bible, a part we call the **Torah**, reflects the light of Jesus. The Torah was written thousands of years before Jesus was born in Bethlehem.

"The Torah talks about Bible heroes such as Jacob, who was a forefather of Jesus, and Moses, the great teacher who received God's laws for His people.

"The Torah says that a Star would someday come forth from the family of Jacob, and that Star was Jesus.

"The Torah also says that someday there would be another great Teacher like Moses, and that great Teacher was Jesus.

"And now we say goodbye to the planet Mercury..."

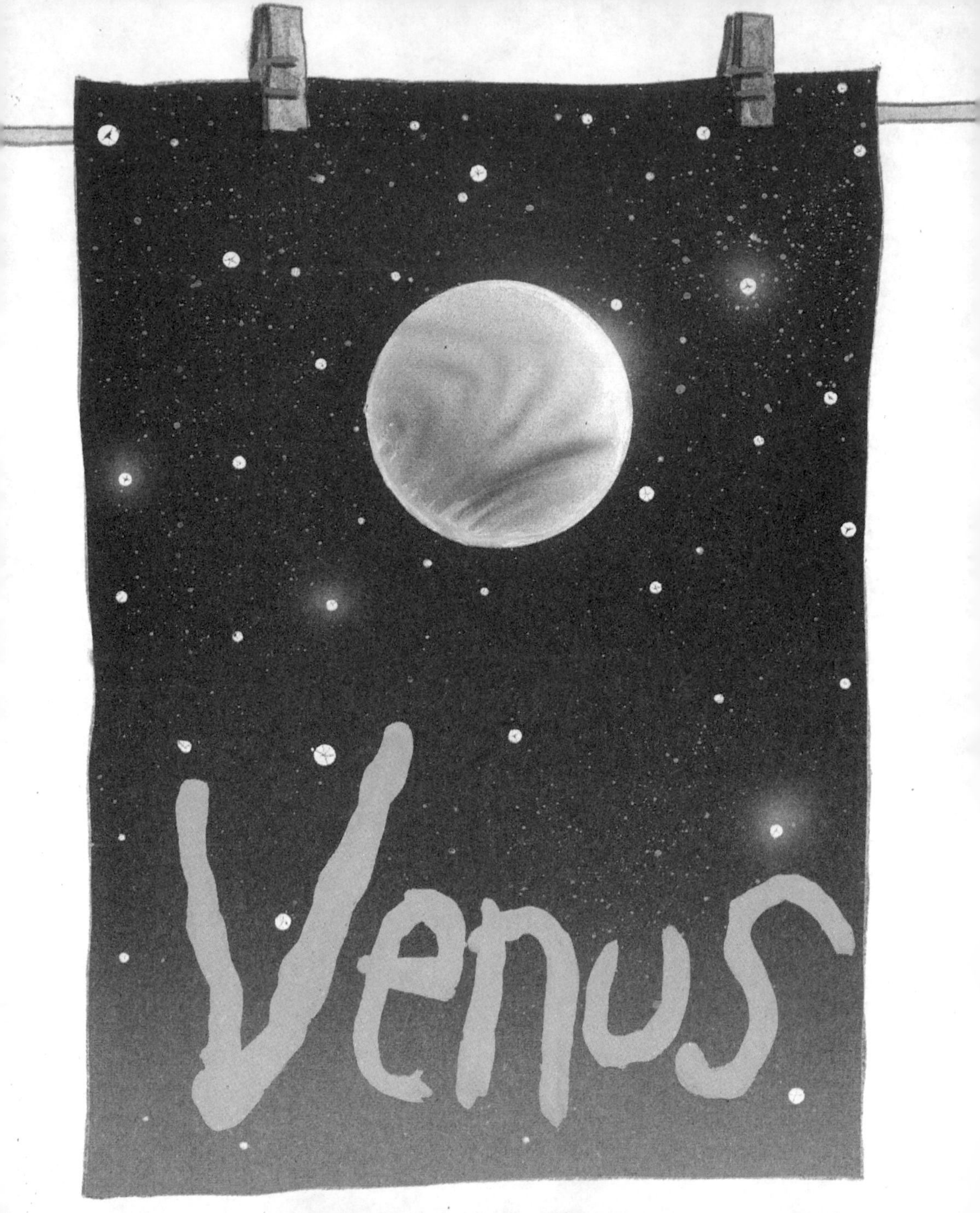
Venus

That was the cue for the children to put a different poster in the window.

"And I see," said Skyler, "that we're already approaching the second planet from the sun, the planet Venus. How do you like this fast spaceship?"

The audience cheered.

"By the way," Skyler said, "the planet Venus has no light of its own. It reflects the light of the sun, and that's why we can see it.

"Venus reminds us of the second part of the Bible, the part we call **History**. This part of the Bible also reflects the light of Jesus.

"Here we meet King David, the great singer and soldier. God promised David that someone in his family would always be King. A thousand years later, Jesus was born into David's family, and He became the King forever.

"And so we say goodbye to Venus…"

"And hello to planet Earth, the beautiful blue planet.

"Earth, as you know, has no light of its own. There's light there only because Earth receives and reflects the light of the sun.

"And so it is with the third part of the Bible, the part we call **Wisdom and Poetry.** In this part of the Bible we find songs written by David and others that are full of the light of Jesus, though they were written a thousand years before He came to earth.

"These songs tell how Jesus would have His hands and feet pierced, which happened when He was nailed to a cross to die. They tell the words that Jesus would cry out from the cross as He was dying: *'My God, My God, why have You forsaken Me?'* And the songs say that Jesus' body would not stay and rot in the grave—and sure enough, Jesus later rose up from the dead, and walked out of His grave after only three days inside.

"And now we leave the blue and beautiful Earth…"

"Mars, the red planet, is next. Mars does not have any light of its own. We can see it only because it reflects the light of the sun.

"And so it is with the fourth part of the Bible, which we call the **Prophets.** The Prophets reflect the light of Jesus Christ, though they were written about 500 years before He came into the world.

"The Prophet Isaiah tells us that a Child would be born, a Son, and that He would be called Wonderful Counselor, Mighty God, Everlasting Father, and Prince of Peace. This Child was Jesus. Isaiah says that He would be born to a virgin mother, and would be the King forever.

"The Prophet Isaiah also tells us that Jesus would suffer and die, in order to carry the punishment for all the wrong things that we have done. He would carry *our* sin and sadness in His own body.

"And now, after Mars, comes the biggest planet of all…"

"Here we are at big, huge Jupiter, which has no light of its own, but reflects the light of the sun. This planet begins a new and different part of the solar system.

"And it reminds us of the part of the Bible called the **Gospels,** which begin a new part of the Bible. Just as Jupiter is the biggest planet, so this part of the Bible gives us the biggest part of the story of Jesus. Here in the Gospels we have the actual account of Jesus coming and living in our world.

"The Gospels tell us that Jesus lived the best and most wonderful life the world has ever seen. He had more love for other people, more patience, more forgiveness, more kindness, and more wisdom than anyone in history. He actually lived a perfect life, never doing one single thing wrong. He could do this because He was God's own Son.

"Then He was killed on a cross. The Gospels tell us that He died to take away the sins of the world.

"Then, the Gospels tell us, Jesus rose up from the dead. He was alive again, and He is alive forever. He's alive at this very moment.

"And so we pass on from the great planet Jupiter…"

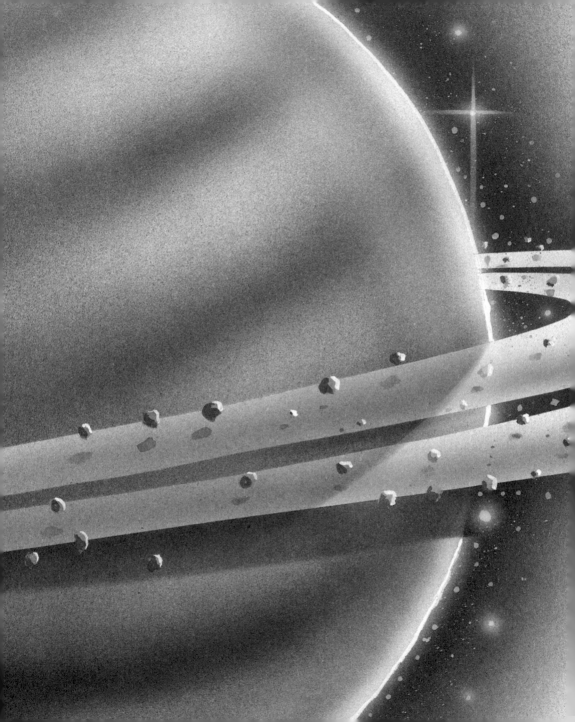

"Next is beautiful Saturn, which also reflects the light of the sun. Saturn is the planet with rings. Saturn reminds us of the part of the Bible called **Acts.** This part of the Bible tells us how Jesus went to heaven to stay until He comes back someday as our King.

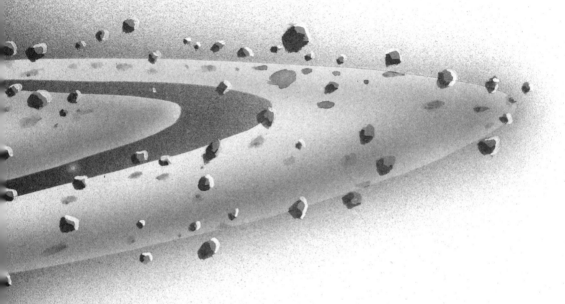

"Acts also tells us how people started taking the good news of Jesus to people all over the world.

"Acts is full of the light of Jesus. It tells how Jesus sent His Spirit to live inside His people, and to circle them with His protection, just like the rings that circle Saturn.

"And now we say goodbye to Saturn and its rings…"

"And we come to the twin planets, Uranus and Neptune, both about the same size. These planets also do not have any light of their own. They reflect the light of the sun.

"Yes, Uranus and Neptune are twins, and the next part of the Bible has two sections that are about the same size too. This part of the Bible is called the **Letters.** It's made up of two groups of letters—one group by a great man named Paul, and the other group by some other men. All these letters were written to help people who had decided to believe in Jesus and to live for Jesus.

"The Letters reflect Jesus because they teach us the meaning of all that Jesus did, and all that He is doing now, and all that He will do in heaven for the people who get to go and live with Him there when they leave this world. The people who get to do this are those who believe in Jesus. And the Letters teach us what it really means to believe in Him.

"After these planets, there is only one more…"

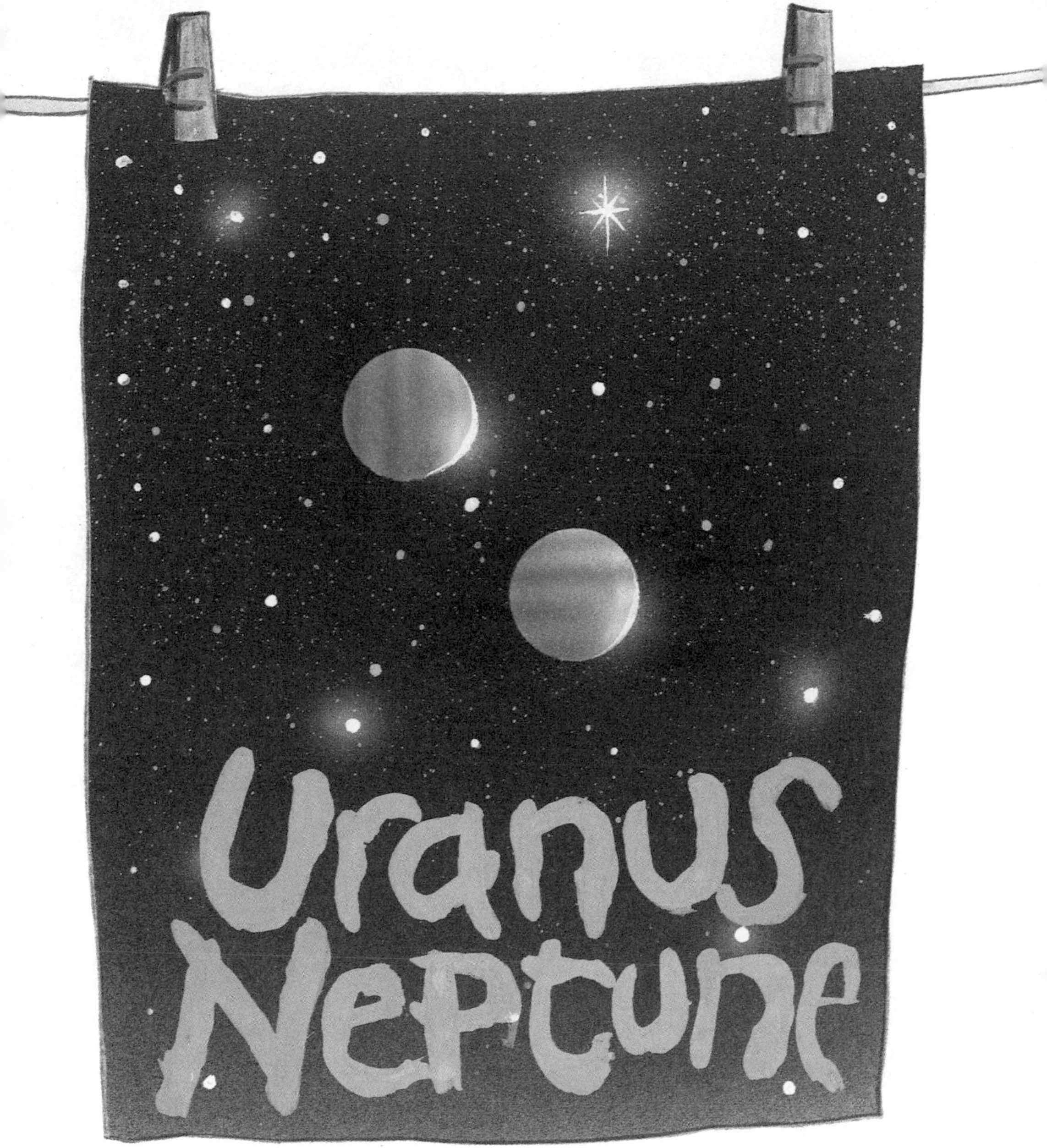
Uranus
Neptune

"And here it is: tiny Pluto, which has no light of its own, but reflects the light of the sun.

"Pluto is the last planet and the smallest planet, and it reminds us of the last and smallest part of the Bible. We call it the **Revelation.**

"Pluto is at the gateway from our solar system to the huge endlessness of outer space beyond. **Revelation** also is at the gateway to the endless beyond, for it tells us about the end of this world, and how Jesus will be the great eternal King of a new kingdom that will go on forever.

"Revelation is full of the light of Jesus. The man who wrote Revelation had a vision, and in that vision he actually saw Jesus in heaven. He tells us that the face of Jesus was as bright as the sun.

"So now we know that of all the things around us that we can see on earth and in the sky, it's the sun that looks most like Jesus.

"Now," said Skyler, "it's time to end our journey. How did you like it?"

The audience cheered.

"Thank you," said Skyler. "Let's all have some lemonade, and we'll talk about it more."

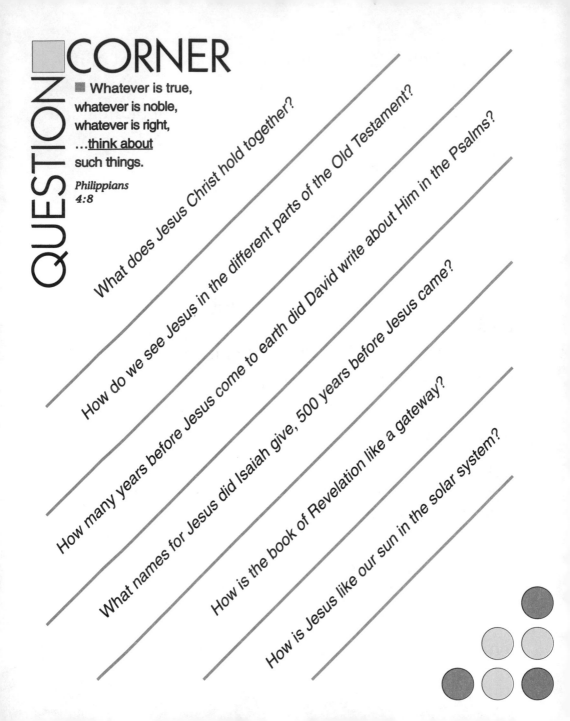

QUESTION CORNER

■ Whatever is true,
whatever is noble,
whatever is right,
…think about
such things.

*Philippians
4:8*

What does Jesus Christ hold together?

How do we see Jesus in the different parts of the Old Testament?

How many years before Jesus come to earth did David write about Him in the Psalms?

What names for Jesus did Isaiah give, 500 years before Jesus came?

How is the book of Revelation like a gateway?

How is Jesus like our sun in the solar system?

"THY WORD IS TRUTH"

DISCOVER
John
17:17

On the night before He died, Jesus prayed that God would make His disciples holy. He wanted them to have the special privilege of knowing they were chosen by God to serve Him. He wanted them to know what it's like to be lifted out of evil, and to be always ready to do good.

Jesus asked God to do this "by the truth." Then Jesus said to God, *"Your word is truth."* It's through the Word of God that we are given the special privilege of serving God and escaping evil.

Earlier that night, Jesus had said, *"I am the way, and <u>the truth</u>, and the life."* The Word of God is truth because it tells about Jesus the Truth.

When Jesus was condemned to die on the cross, Governor Pilate asked Him, "What is truth?" Pilate's heart was too blind to see that Truth was standing right before his eyes!

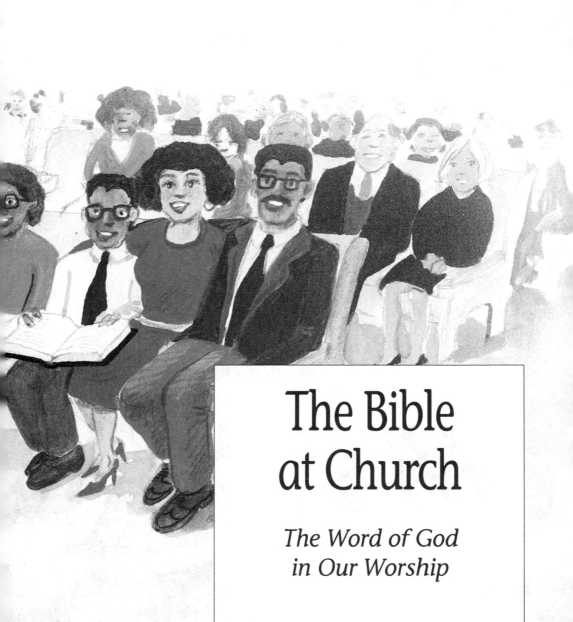

The Bible at Church

The Word of God in Our Worship

21 The next Sunday was "Bible Celebration Day" at church. The pastor had asked Skyler, Ian, Nancie, Jackson, and Krista to lead the people during the worship time.

They were glad when they saw such a big crowd. Even Reggie Longman and his family were there.

As the service began, Skyler played the piano while everyone sang. They sang these lines, and many more:

> *Holy Bible, book divine,*
> *precious treasure, thou art mine....*

> *Sing them over again to me,*
> *wonderful words of life!*
> *Let me more of their beauty see,*
> *wonderful words of life!...*

> *Jesus loves me! This I know,*
> *for the Bible tells me so....*

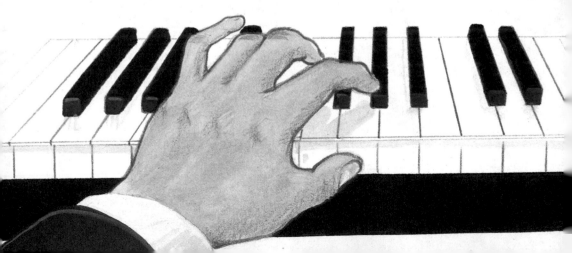

Standing on the promises that cannot fail,
    when the howling storms of doubt and fear assail;
by the living Word of God I shall prevail,
    standing on the promises of God!…

        How firm a foundation, ye saints of the Lord,
          is laid for your faith in His excellent Word!

Then Skyler got up and said this: "God has done GREAT THINGS. And He has written a GREAT BOOK to tell us about them. The GREATEST THING God has done for us was to send Jesus to our world.

"Jesus did beautiful miracles here. Perhaps we would all be in tears if we'd been there to see them. We would catch the joy on the faces of those who had been blind all their lives, but who now could see. We would watch tearful parents embracing children who were fevered or crippled or dying or dead, but who now were alive and healthy by a touch from the hand of Jesus.

"Yes, His miracles were beautiful. And *just as beautiful* are the words He spoke, the words written for us in our Bible.

"They're just common words, words you and I use every day. But from the mouth of God, they ring out with power and truth."

Later, Jackson stood in front and lit a candle. And he said, "The Bible is a light for us because the Bible is all about Jesus. And Jesus says, *'I am the light of the world.'*

"Our world is filled with much darkness. But we don't have to stay in that darkness. We can choose light if we want to. We find that light in the Bible.

"Psalm 119:105 tells us that God's Word is a light for our path. And why did God give us His light? Because He loves us. God's Word comes straight from His heart.

"I've written a song about this," Jackson continued, "and you can join me in singing it, to the tune of 'He's Got the Whole World in His Hands.'"

Skyler played along on the piano while they sang:

He wrote the whole Bible...from His heart;
He wrote the Holy Bible...from His heart;
He wrote the whole Bible...from His heart;
He wrote the Bible from His heart!

He wants the whole Bible...in my heart;
He wants the Holy Bible...in my heart;
He wants the whole Bible...in my heart;
He wants the Bible in my heart!

Then Krista stood before the people. With her words and the motions of her hands, she told the famous story that Jesus told about a man who built his house on a rock, and another who built his house on sand.

"Then a terrible storm came," Krista said, "with a mighty wind…a pounding rain…and a rising flood.

"The house built on sand fell, with a CRASH! But the house built on rock stayed firm.

"Jesus then said this: When we hear God's Words but *don't do them,* it's like building our house on sand instead of rock.

"To really learn the Bible," Krista said, "doesn't mean simply piling up more and more facts about the Bible in my mind. It doesn't mean simply memorizing more verses. It doesn't mean knowing more names of Bible heroes and what each one did. It doesn't mean knowing more big Bible words like *redemption* and *righteousness* and *repentance* and *resurrection.*

"Lots of people down through history have known tons *about* the Bible, but it made no difference in the way they lived. And that's not right. No, Nancie and Jackson and Ian and I have been learning that Bible knowledge is just the beginning. It works like this:

"First we find out what the Bible says. We read and study and think about it.

"Then we pray for God to help us understand it. God's Holy Spirit gives us that help.

"Last and greatest of all, we *do* what the Bible says. And when we do, our lives will change. Each of us will be a growing person and a better person."

Nancie came up next. "I love music," she said. "And I love verse 54 in Psalm 119, which says this: *'No matter where I go and live, God's Word will always be the theme of my song.'*

"As I play a melody on the flute for you this morning, God's Word is the theme of my song. It's a melody of joy, because I'm so glad for the things I've been learning about the Bible."

Then Ian came forward. "I'll let the Bible speak for itself," he said, "as I read from Psalm 19:

"The Lord's teachings are perfect.
They give new strength.
The Lord's rules can be trusted.
They make plain people wise.
The Lord's orders are right.
They make people happy.
The Lord's commands are pure.
They light up the way....
They are worth more than gold,
even the purest gold.
They are sweeter than honey,
even the finest honey.
They tell us what to do.
Keeping them brings great reward.

"These pure and perfect and sweet words," Ian said, "are the words of the Bible. And these are the teachings that we sing about, and pray about, and learn about when we come together in church.

"Please pray with me now:

"Lord God our Father, all of us here today want to be strong and wise and happy. We want the great reward that You promise us if we keep Your commands. Please help us keep them. And thank You for giving us a great Book that's so rich and right, and that tells us all about You. I pray this in Jesus' name. Amen."

QUESTION CORNER

■ Whatever is true,
whatever is noble,
whatever is right,
...think about
such things.

*Philippians
4:8*

What songs about the Bible do you know?

Why does God give us "light for our path" in the Bible?

Can you tell all of the story that Krista told in church on Bible Celebration Day?

Why do you think Jesus told that story of the men who built on sand and on rock?

What steps should we follow to truly learn the Bible?

What did Ian pray in church that day?

"A LIGHT FOR MY PATH"

Have you ever been outside on a very dark night, and forgotten to take a flashlight? Your feet may have told you first how badly you needed one —when they ran into a rock or a hole or a cat, or perhaps something worse!

In Bible times there were no flashlights, no electric lights of any kind. But then as now, people had the best light of all. Psalm 119:105 tells what it is: *"Your word is a lamp to my feet and a light for my path."*

God has a different path for each person to take in life. He's planned something different for each of us to do. But *everyone's* path leads at times through shadows and darkness.

God knows we'll need a light for our path—and He's given us that light in His Word.

In the Air Over There

*An Eagle's-Eye Look
at the Land of the Bible*

22 For what must have been the fortieth time since leaving New York, Nancie said, "I have to pinch myself to believe this is happening!" Skyler and Mrs. Brown, Nancie, Krista, Jackson, and Ian had just flown halfway around the world, all the way from America to the Holy Land—the Land of the Bible! It was a long, tiring trip of many hours. But with all their excitement, no one felt like sleeping yet tonight—their first night in Jerusalem, the Holy City.

The trip had been paid for by a man and his wife in their church. They were the owners of a travel agency.

"We were so encouraged by your big part in our Bible Celebration service," the man said, "that we would like to send you to the place where it all happened. We believe this is what God wants us to do."

Arrangements were quickly made for the children to miss several days of school. And now, after whirlwind days of packing and planning, they were here!

They finally got to bed, slept late the next morning, then got their first look at Jerusalem by daylight.

There was so much to see, and they saw much of it that first day. The sight that most impressed Ian was an ancient tomb cut out of rock. To seal the entrance, it had a great round stone like a wheel that could be rolled into place. It was probably much like the tomb in which Jesus lay until that first Easter Sunday. As they all looked at it, Skyler read from the Bible: *"There was a violent earthquake, for an angel of the Lord came down from heaven and, going to the tomb, rolled back the stone and sat on it. His appearance was like lightning, and his clothes were white as snow…"*

As he thought about that mighty morning, Ian could almost feel the earth shake under his feet, and he could imagine seeing the angel. Jesus had been carried into His tomb as a body, beaten up and dead. But with all the power of God, He rose up, alive forevermore! The tomb was empty! Ian felt the truth of it as never before. He felt like shouting it: *Jesus is alive!*

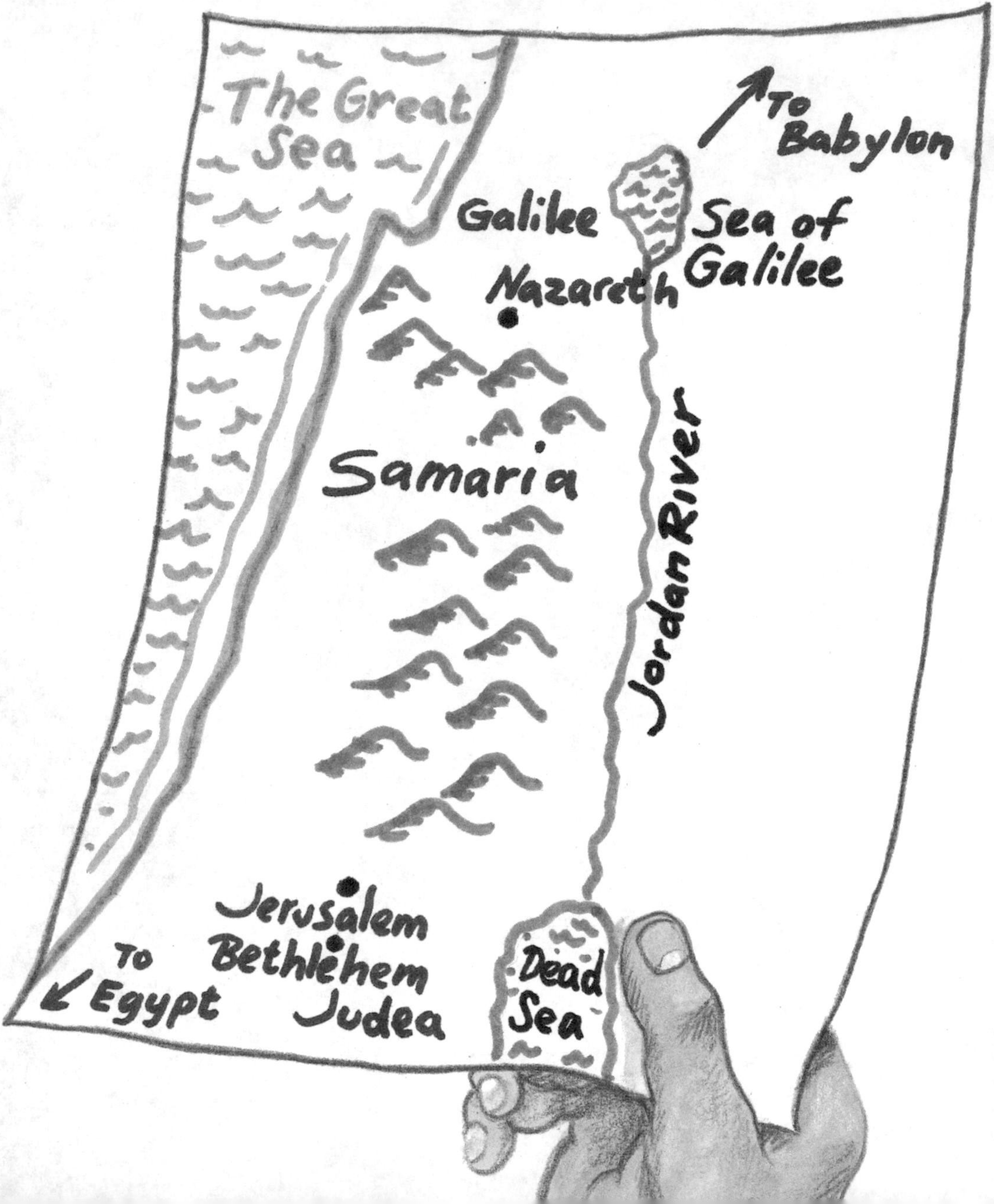

The Great Sea
To Babylon
Galilee
Sea of Galilee
Nazareth
Samaria
Jordan River
Jerusalem
Bethlehem
Judea
To Egypt
Dead Sea

That evening Skyler showed the children a map he had just drawn. He had been able to rent a private jet ("I'm very thankful for that," he told them). With Skyler as pilot, they would take off tomorrow morning from the Jerusalem airport to fly over places in Israel where Jesus had lived and worked.

"Bethlehem is nearby, so we'll fly over it first," Skyler said. "It's a great starting point, since Jesus was born there. Then we'll go north to Nazareth where Jesus grew up. We'll come back south along the Jordan River, where He was baptized, and fly over the Dead Sea and the Wilderness of Judea. That's where Jesus spent forty days fasting, and where Satan tempted Him before Jesus started His ministry.

"Then we'll head north again," Skyler said, "this time to the beautiful Sea of Galilee, in the middle of the territory where Jesus did so much of His teaching and healing. After that we'll move south once more, and come back to Jerusalem. There's lots more for us to see here."

The next morning was another sunny day in Israel —and great for flying.

They were over Bethlehem, the city of David, in just a matter of minutes. Krista was struck with how small it was. She began humming *O Little Town of Bethlehem* to herself.

They had a Bible with them, to read from at each place they came to. Skyler asked Krista to read first. He had prepared a list of reference numbers for the verses to look up. Krista spoke aloud the Bethlehem passages as she found each one: "1 Chronicles 11:16-19— *'David was in a protected place at that time. The Philistine army was staying in the town of Bethlehem. David had a strong desire for some water. He said, "Oh, I wish someone would get me water from the well near the city gate of Bethlehem!" So David's Three Mighty Men fought their way through the Philistine army. And they took water out of the well near the city gate in Bethlehem. Then they took it back to David.'*

"Micah 5:3—*'You, Bethlehem Ephrathah, are one of the smallest towns in Judah. But from you will come one who will rule Israel for me. He comes from very old times, from days long ago.'*

"And from Luke 2: *'Joseph went to the town of Beth-lehem in Judea. This town was known as the town of David. Joseph went there because he was from the family of David.... While Joseph and Mary were in Bethlehem, the time came for her to have the baby. She gave birth to her first son. There were no rooms left in the inn. So she wrapped the baby with cloths and laid him in a box where animals are fed.*

"'*That night, some shepherds were in the fields nearby watching their sheep. An angel of the Lord stood before them.... The angel said to them, "Don't be afraid, because I am bringing you some good news. It will be a joy to all the people. Today your Savior was born in David's town. He is Christ the Lord."'*"

In another few minutes, Skyler said, "There's Nazareth!"

"Already?" said Jackson. "Man, this country isn't very big."

"No, it isn't," agreed Skyler. "Will you read our Nazareth verses, Jackson?"

Jackson read them: "From Luke 2: *'Jesus went with Mary and Joseph to Nazareth and obeyed them. His mother was still thinking about all that had happened. Jesus continued to learn more and more and to grow physically. People liked him, and he pleased God.'*

"And from John 1: *'Philip found Nathanael and told him, "Remember that Moses wrote in the law about a man who was coming, and the prophets also wrote about him. We have found him. He is Jesus, the son of Joseph. He is from Nazareth." But Nathanael said to Philip, "Nazareth! Can anything good come from Nazareth?" Philip answered, "Come and see."'*"

Later, as they came over the Jordan River, Nancie took the Bible and read. "From Mark 1: *'At that time Jesus came from the town of Nazareth in Galilee to the place where John was. John baptized Jesus in the Jordan River. When Jesus was coming up out of the water, he saw heaven open. The Holy Spirit came down on him like a dove. A voice came from heaven and said, "You are my Son and I love you. I am very pleased with you."'"*

Next they were over the Wilderness of Judea, beside the Dead Sea. Skyler quoted from memory a part of Luke 4:

"Jesus, full of the Holy Spirit, returned from the Jordan and was led by the Spirit in the desert, where for forty days he was tempted by the devil. He ate nothing during those days, and at the end of them he was hungry.

The devil said to him, 'If you are the Son of God, tell this stone to become bread.' Jesus answered, 'It is written: "Man does not live on bread alone."'"

When they were over the Sea of Galilee, Ian read
from the Gospel of Mark:

"*After John was put in prison, Jesus went into Galilee and
preached the Good News from God. Jesus said, 'The right
time has come. The kingdom of God is near. Change your
hearts and lives and believe the Good News!'*

"*When Jesus was walking by Lake Galilee, he saw Simon
and Simon's brother, Andrew. They were fishermen and were
throwing a net into the lake to catch fish. Jesus said to them,
'Come and follow me. I will make you fishermen for men.'*

"So Simon and Andrew immediately left their nets and followed him.

"Jesus continued walking by Lake Galilee. He saw two more brothers, James and John, the sons of Zebedee. They were in their boat, preparing their nets to catch fish. Their father Zebedee and the men who worked for him were in the boat with the brothers. When Jesus saw the brothers, he called them to come with him. They left their father and followed Jesus."

Now they were approaching Jerusalem, and Skyler asked them to imagine what it might have looked like centuries ago when Jesus came to the city.

Nancie read from the Psalms and from Luke:

"Jerusalem, we are standing at your gates. Jerusalem is built as a city where friends can come together. The people from the tribes go up there.... It is the rule to praise the Lord at Jerusalem.... Pray for peace in Jerusalem...."

"Jesus came near Jerusalem. He saw the city and began to cry for it. Jesus said to Jerusalem, 'I wish you knew today what would bring you peace! But you can't know it, because it is hidden from you. A time is coming when your enemies will build a wall around you and will hold you in on all sides. They will destroy you and all your people. Not one stone of your buildings will be left on another. All this will happen because you did not know the time when God came to save you."

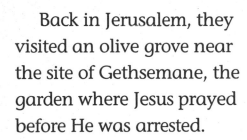

Back in Jerusalem, they visited an olive grove near the site of Gethsemane, the garden where Jesus prayed before He was arrested.

Krista read the story from the Gospel of Mark:

"Jesus and his followers went to a place called Gethsemane. He said to his followers, 'Sit here while I pray.' Jesus told Peter, James, and John to come with him.

"Then Jesus began to be very sad and troubled. He said to them, 'I am full of sorrow. My heart is breaking with sadness. Stay here and watch.' Jesus walked a little farther away from them. Then he fell on the ground and prayed. He prayed that, if possible, he would not have this time of suffering. He prayed, 'Abba, Father! You can do all things. Let me not have this cup of suffering. But do what you want, not what I want.'"

Next Skyler and Mrs. Brown and the children visited a hill in Jerusalem that had markings like a skull. Some thought it might have been the hill on which Jesus was crucified.

Jackson read from the Scriptures:

"They led Jesus to the place called Golgotha. (Golgotha means the Place of the Skull.) At Golgotha the soldiers tried to give Jesus wine to drink. This wine was mixed with myrrh. But he refused to drink it. The soldiers nailed Jesus to a cross.... It was nine o'clock in the morning when they nailed Jesus to the cross....

"They also put two robbers on crosses beside Jesus, one on the right, and the other on the left. People walked by and insulted Jesus. They shook their heads, saying... 'Save your-self! Come down from that cross!'...

"At noon the whole country became dark. This darkness lasted for three hours. At three o'clock Jesus cried in a loud voice, 'My God, my God, why have you left me alone?'...

"Then Jesus cried in a loud voice and died.... The army officer who was standing there before the cross saw what happened when Jesus died. The officer said, 'This man really was the Son of God!'"

23 The next day they walked over to the area in Jerusalem where the Temple once stood. Mrs. Brown took a picture of Skyler and the children. Then she read from the book of Acts:

"One day Peter and John went to the Temple. It was three o'clock in the afternoon. This was the time for the daily prayer service. There, at the Temple gate called Beautiful Gate, was a man who had been crippled all his life. Every day he was carried to this gate to beg. He would ask for money from the people going into the Temple.

"The man saw Peter and John going into the Temple and asked them for money. Peter and John looked straight at him and said, 'Look at us!'

"The man looked at them; he thought they were going to give him some money. But Peter said, 'I don't have any silver or gold, but I do have something else I can give you: By the power of Jesus Christ from Nazareth—stand up and walk!'

"Then Peter took the man's right hand and lifted him up. Immediately the man's feet and ankles became strong. He jumped up, stood on his feet, and began to walk. He went into the Temple with them, walking and jumping, and praising God."

Ephesus

Euphrates
River

Tigris River

the Great
Sea

Sea of Galilee

Jerusalem   Babylon

Dead Sea

SINAI

Egypt   the Great Desert

After they heard that, the children all began jumping and running on the ancient stones. They imagined what it was like for that crippled man to be able to jump and run for the *very first time.*

When they were out of breath, Skyler showed them another map. They were going on another trip in the jet, this time to places that were farther away from Jerusalem: Egypt, the ruins of ancient Babylon, and the ruins of Ephesus, the city where the apostle Paul stayed for quite a while.

They would leave the next morning — the beginning of their last full day in the Holy Land.

First they flew over Egypt. Skyler pointed to the Great Pyramids and said, "Those were standing — and were already old—when Moses grew up in Egypt more than 3,000 years ago."

Ian read from the book of Exodus: *"The people of Israel had lived in Egypt for 430 years. On the day the 430 years ended, the Lord's divisions of people left Egypt. That night the Lord kept watch to bring them out of Egypt. ...All the Israelites did just as the Lord had commanded Moses and Aaron. Then on that same day, the Lord led the Israelites out of Egypt."*

Then they flew over Sinai, the rugged wilderness between Egypt and Israel, where the people of Israel wandered for forty years before they took over the Promised Land.

"And it was down there," Skyler said, "on Mount Sinai, where God gave the Ten Commandments to Moses and all the people."

Nancie read about it, again from Exodus:

"The Israelites camped in the desert in front of Mount Sinai. Then Moses went up on the mountain to God. The Lord called to him from the mountain. The Lord said, 'Say this to the family of Jacob. And tell this to the people of Israel: Every one of you has seen what I did to the people of Egypt. You saw how I carried you out of Egypt. I did it as an eagle carries her young on her wings. And I brought you here to me. So now obey me and keep my agreement. Do this, and you will be my own possession, chosen from all nations. Even though the whole earth is mine, you will be my kingdom of priests. You will be a nation that belongs to me alone.'"

As they came closer to Israel, Skyler pointed out
Mount Nebo below them. "Just before Moses died, God
brought him up on this mountain, and from the top he
could see all the Promised Land stretching out below."

Krista read from Deuteronomy 34: *"Then Moses
climbed up Mount Nebo.... From there the Lord showed him
all the land. He could see from Gilead to Dan. He could see
all of Naphtali and the lands of Ephraim and Manasseh. He
could see all the land of Judah as far as the Great Sea...."*

"Then the Lord said to Moses, 'This is the land I promised to Abraham, Isaac and Jacob. I said to them, "I will give this land to your descendants." I have let you look at it, Moses. But you will not cross over there.'

"Then Moses, the servant of the Lord, died there in Moab. It was as the Lord had said. The Lord buried Moses in Moab…. But even today no one knows where his grave is. Moses was 120 years old when he died. His eyes were not weak. And he was still strong."

Skyler lifted the jet higher, and they flew across Israel and on toward the ruins of the ancient city of Babylon. On the way there, Skyler told them how big and strong the city once was. It was the greatest city in the world, and the capital of the empire that destroyed Jerusalem and captured God's people. As the jet came near the place, the children could imagine what Babylon once looked like, in the days of her glory.

Jackson read from the book of Daniel: *"Twelve months after the dream which Daniel explained to him, King Nebuchadnezzar was walking on the roof of his palace in Babylon. And he said, 'Look at Babylon. I built this great city. It is my palace. I built this great place by my power to show how great I am.'*

"The words were still in his mouth when a voice came from heaven. The voice said, 'King Nebuchadnezzar, these things will happen to you: Your royal power has been taken away from you. You will be forced away from people. You will live with the wild animals. You will be fed grass like an oxen. Seven years will pass before you learn this lesson: The Most High God rules over the kingdoms of men. And the Most High God gives those kingdoms to anyone he wants.'"

From Babylon, Skyler swung the jet on a westward course. They passed over the city of Tarsus, where the apostle Paul was from. They also passed over many of the cities where Paul and his helpers started churches.

Passing over the city of Ephesus, they saw the ruins of a great theater where Paul almost caused a riot. The children and Skyler read the story together in Acts 19. Ephesus had a temple to the goddess Artemis. The men who made money by making and selling little silver images of Artemis did not like it when Paul began getting people to worship Christ instead of Artemis. The workers in silver became angry and gathered a huge, shouting mob into the theater. Paul tried to go in and talk to them, but his friends were afraid for his life, and wouldn't let him enter. It took several hours for the crowd to quieten down and go home. "This was just one of many commotions that seemed to happen wherever Paul went," said Skyler. "It was an exciting time for Christians everywhere. By reading about these things in the Bible, it's easier to remember how God wants our Christian life to be exciting, not dull."

"You've helped make it more exciting for *us,* Captain Skyler," said Nancie.

"That's for sure," said Jackson. "Thank you for getting the Bible to start talking to me."

"You're welcome," answered Skyler with a grin. "I'm glad I had a part in that. And I know the best excitement in your Christian life is still to come, if you keep listening to what God tells you day by day in His Word."

Skyler turned the jet toward Jerusalem, where they would spend their last night before going home.

"Captain Skyler," said Krista, "how do we make sure we're listening to God when we're in the Bible?"

"First, of course," said Skyler, "is to pray for His help through the Holy Spirit. Then watch for His **commands** in Scripture that will guide you on the right path. Keep looking for **promises** from God that you can believe and thank Him for. Look for **prayers** on the Bible's pages that you can pray for yourself. And look at the people in the Bible—look for **good examples** you can follow, and **bad examples** that warn you about what *not* to do.

"It's all there, waiting for you and me...."

QUESTION CORNER

Whatever is true,
whatever is noble,
whatever is right,
...think about
such things.

*Philippians
4:8*

What do you know about Bethlehem and Nazareth?

Where was Jesus baptized? Where was He tempted by the devil?

What happened on Mount Sinai? What happened on Mount Nebo?

Which places in the Holy Land would you most like to visit?

How can we make sure we're listening to God in the Bible?

How do you like this book?

Taking a Look, Book by Book

Highlights of ALL the Bible's Books

SUPER TRUTH
in the Bible

The first two chapters of the Bible—**Genesis 1 and 2**—
tell us about the perfect paradise enjoyed by
the first man and woman God created.

The last two chapters of the Bible—**Revelation 21 and 22**—
tell us about the NEW perfect paradise God is creating for
His chosen people from throughout the world's history.

All the Bible chapters in between—the 1,187 chapters
from Genesis 3 through Revelation 20—tell us this:

1. How the first man and woman lost that first paradise;

2. How God put a plan into action for getting men
    and women into the *new* paradise, where they will
    live forever. This plan has taken thousands of
    years to unfold.

This is the story of mankind…

And it is *your* story and *my* story too!

The Bible is like a rose. In the <u>Old Testament</u> the flower is only a bud. It is opening very slowly.

In the <u>New Testament</u> the flower has finally opened into a full bloom, beautiful in color and fragrance.

But both are the same flower!

The Old Testament and the New Testament give us *the same message:* God, in His love, saves us from our sin through His Son, Jesus Christ. In the Old Testament this message only gradually becomes clear. In the New Testament the message is fully opened, and all its rich beauty is there for us to know.

TORAH (or LAW)

Genesis

● <u>**What's BIG in This Book**</u>: *Beginnings*—the beginning of the world, the beginning of all animals and plants, the beginning of men and women, the beginning of human sin, and the beginning of God's plan to save us from that sin. This book focuses on people, and not on science and the universe, because people are more important to God than nature and the universe are.

➤ <u>**What to Look For**</u>: How God made promises to Noah, and to three men in one family—Abraham, Isaac, and Jacob. Look also at the amazing ways God protected and honored Jacob's son Joseph.

★ <u>**KEY VERSE**</u>: *"So God created human beings in his image. In the image of God he created them. He created them male and female"* (1:27).

■ <u>**Background**</u>: Moses wrote this book, as well as the other four books in the Torah.

Exodus

● <u>**What's BIG in This Book**</u>: God's amazing *rescue* of the Hebrew people out of cruel slavery in Egypt, and how He started them on their way toward a new land. This book is filled with the mightiest collection of God's miracles in the entire Old Testament. It also includes the Ten Commandments.

➤ <u>**What to Look For**</u>: The *reason* God did what He did in bringing the Hebrews out of Egypt. Look also for the *reason* God gave them the Ten Commandments and other laws after the Hebrews came out of Egypt. Notice as well how God kept the promises He made earlier to Abraham, Isaac, and Jacob. Look for God's love in every chapter.

★ <u>**KEY VERSE**</u>: *"Don't be afraid! Stand still and see the Lord save you today.... The Lord will fight for you"* (14:13-14).

■ <u>**Background**</u>: The word *Exodus* means "exit."

● **What's BIG in This Book**: *God's laws.* These laws taught the Hebrew people to be holy, especially in the way they worshiped God—the most important thing in anyone's life.

Leviticus

➤ **What to Look For**: When you read about all the blood sacrifices in Leviticus, look for the *reason* behind them. And let them remind you of how Christ had to shed His blood as the sacrifice to save *us* from our sin. Leviticus will help you be more serious about God's hatred for sin, and His desire for us to be "clean" in our hearts.

★ **KEY VERSE:** *"The LORD said to Moses, 'Tell all the people of Israel: I am the Lord your God. You must be holy because I am holy'"* (19:1-2).

■ **Background**: This book continues the story of Moses' life and work. His story is longer than anyone else's in the Bible, except for that of Jesus Himself.

Aaron's sons Nadab and Abihu ...did not use the special fire Moses had commanded them to use. So fire came down from the Lord and destroyed Nadab and Abihu. They died in front of the Lord. Then Moses said to Aaron, "This is what the Lord was speaking about when he said, 'I must be respected as holy by those who come near me.'"

—LEVITICUS 10:1-3

The Lord sent a strong wind from the sea. It blew quail into the area all around the camp. The quail were about three feet above the ground. There were quail a day's walk in any direction. The people went out and gathered quail.

—NUMBERS 11:31-32

Numbers

● **What's BIG in This Book**: *Numbers.* The Hebrew people were counted twice in this book. The huge number of the people and their fighting men helps us see God's power in leading and protecting them in a desert for forty years. Those forty years had plenty of excitement, as this book shows us.

➤ **What to Look For**: How God responded to all the grumbling He heard from the Hebrew people. Look also at how God tested them, to let them see for themselves how much more they needed to love Him. As you read, ask yourself this: How is God training and testing *me?*

★ **KEY VERSE**: *"May the Lord bless you and keep you. May the Lord show you his kindness. May he have mercy on you. May the Lord watch over you and give you peace"* (6:24-26).

■ **Background**: The Hebrew title for this book means "In the Desert."

● **What's BIG in This Book:** *Remembering.* In this book we read what Moses told the Hebrew

people to remember, as they prepared to enter the Promised Land. We also see how important it is to obey God—for our own good.

➤ **What to Look For:** What God expects from His people, and *why.* Notice how much God loved Israel. And especially in the last four chapters, notice how much Moses loved God, as he spoke his last words before dying and being buried by God Himself. As you read, ask yourself this: What does God want *me* to remember and obey?

★ **KEY VERSE:** *"Listen, people of Israel! The Lord is our God. He is the only Lord. Love the Lord your God with all your heart, soul and strength. Always remember these commands I give you today"* (6:4-6).

■ **Background:** The Ten Commandments are repeated in this book.

Words for the War against the Devil

When Satan tempted Jesus three times in the desert, Jesus answered each time with words from the book of Deuteronomy.

When Satan told Him to turn rocks into bread, Jesus said, "It is written in the Scriptures, 'A person does not live only by eating bread. But a person lives by everything the Lord says'" (Deuteronomy 8:3).

When Satan told Him to jump off the top of the temple, Jesus said, "It is written in the Scriptures, 'Do not test the Lord your God'" (Deuteronomy 6:16).

And when Satan said, "Bow down and worship me," Jesus answered, "Go away from me, Satan! It is written in the Scriptures, 'You must worship the Lord your God. Serve only him!'" (Deuteronomy 6:13). And with that, Satan left Him.

God's Word is "the sword of the Spirit" (Ephesians 6:17). Remember to use it as Jesus did to fight against the devil's attacks.

HISTORY

Joshua

● **What's BIG in This Book:** *Victory* for God's people in taking over the Promised Land. Joshua was their leader in this victory, and his life is a great example of godly leadership.

➤ **What to Look For:** How God kept His promises made so long before to Abraham, Isaac, and Jacob. Look also for why Joshua was a good leader, and why Israel was able to take over the Promised Land. What lessons can you find in this book for how *we* can live a life of victory over sin and the devil today?

★ **KEY VERSE:** *"Joshua, be strong and brave! You must lead these people so they can take their land.... Be strong and brave. Be sure to obey all the teachings my servant Moses gave you. If you follow them exactly, you will be successful in everything you do"* (1:6-7).

■ **Background:** Joshua's name in Hebrew means the same as *Jesus*.

Judges

● **What's BIG in This Book:** The *sadness* of turning away from God. In the book of Joshua, the story of Israel in the Promised Land is one of faith, victory, joy, and strength. But in the book of Judges, the story is mostly one of unbelief, defeat, sadness, and weakness.

➤ **What to Look For:** The terrible consequences of sin. Enjoy the bright spots in the book: When God sent leaders (sometimes called "judges") to rescue the people for a time from their enemies. These heroes include Deborah, Gideon, and Samson.

★ **KEY VERSE:** *"After those people died, their children grew up. They did not know the Lord or what he had done for Israel. So they did evil and worshiped the Baal idols. They did what the Lord said was wrong"* (2:10-11).

■ **Background:** This book includes about 350 years of history.

● <u>**What's BIG in This Book**</u>: A story of *love* and *loyalty*. It's especially beautiful because it takes place during the dark years of sadness described in the book of Judges.

> <u>**What to Look For**</u>: Look for wisdom, goodness, and kindness in all three of the major characters in this story: Ruth; her mother-in-law, Naomi; and Boaz, the man who became Ruth's husband. How did God show His tender care for Ruth, Naomi, and Boaz? And notice how love and loyalty opened the door from sadness to joy for Naomi and Ruth. How can you follow their example?

★ <u>**KEY VERSE**</u>: *"Every place you go, I will go. Every place you live, I will live. Your people will be my people. Your God will be my God"* (1:16).

■ <u>**Background**</u>: Ruth became the great-grandmother of King David.

> **Ruth**

Boaz said to Ruth, "Bring me your shawl. Now, hold it open." So Ruth held her shawl open, and Boaz poured six portions of barley into it. Boaz then put it on her back, and she went to the city.

—RUTH 3:15

1 Samuel

● **What's BIG in This Book**: Israel's *king*.

➤ **What to Look For**: How some people are strong
and brave, and others are weak. Many people are important in this
story of how Israel became a nation with a king: Hannah, Samuel,
Eli, Saul, Jonathan, David. Get to know each one, and look for
strengths which you would like God to build into *your* life.

★ **KEY VERSE**: *"God does not see the same way people see. People look
at the outside of a person, but the Lord looks at the heart"* (16:7).

■ **Background**: 1 and 2 Samuel at first were only one book, and
they were also sometimes combined with 1 and 2 Kings.

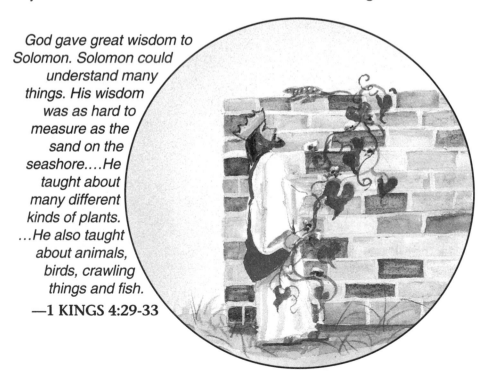

*God gave great wisdom to
Solomon. Solomon could
understand many
things. His wisdom
was as hard to
measure as the
sand on the
seashore....He
taught about
many different
kinds of plants.
...He also taught
about animals,
birds, crawling
things and fish.*

—1 KINGS 4:29-33

● **What's BIG in This Book**: God's hand on the life of *David,* Israel's greatest king; and David's true love for the Lord.

2 Samuel

➤ **What to Look For:** How David followed God and pleased God, even after he had to admit making great mistakes.

★ **KEY VERSE:** *"David knew the Lord really had made him king of Israel. And he knew the Lord had made his kingdom very important"* (5:12).

■ **Background:** As in all the Bible, this book gives us an honest picture of its hero. We see David's weaknesses, as well as his strengths.

● **What's BIG in This Book**: The rule of *Solomon* the king, and later, the greatness of *Elijah* the prophet. In the middle of this book, Israel was split into two kingdoms—all because of the disobedience of Solomon and the foolishness of his son.

1 Kings

➤ **What to Look For:** Learn especially from the life of Elijah how to stand up for God when others will not stand with you.

★ **KEY VERSE:** *"You must serve me as your father David did. He was fair and sincere. You must obey my laws and do everything I command"* (9:4).

■ **Background:** 1 and 2 Kings were originally part of one book.

● **What's BIG in This Book**: The long story of how God's people were defeated and led into *captivity.*

2 Kings

➤ **What to Look For:** God's patience in giving His people warnings and "second chances" to do what was right. But they wouldn't listen and obey, so God sent a final, terrible punishment.

★ **KEY VERSE:** *"The Lord used every prophet and seer to warn Israel and Judah. He said, 'Stop your evil ways. Obey my commands and laws....' But the people would not listen. They were stubborn..."* (17:13-14).

■ **Background:** Of the 39 kings in these two books, 30 were evil.

THE OLD TESTAMENT, Book by Book ●●● *361*

1 Chronicles

● **What's BIG in This Book**: The greatness and godliness of *David the king.*

➤ **What to Look For**: David's desire to worship the Lord, and to build a temple in Jerusalem for Him.

★ **KEY VERSE**: *"David did what God commanded him to do.... So David became famous in all the countries. And the Lord made all nations afraid of David"* (14:16-17).

■ **Background**: 1 and 2 Chronicles were at first only one book. They return to the same history which we find in 1 and 2 Samuel and 1 and 2 Kings. But the writer of Chronicles carefully chooses certain parts of that history to tell us about, and ignores other parts. For example, after the kingdom was split following Solomon's death, the Chronicles focus only on the kings of Judah, the southern kingdom.

2 Chronicles

● **What's BIG in This Book**: The *Temple* built by Solomon, and how the Temple (and all Jerusalem) was destroyed when later kings would not obey God.

➤ **What to Look For**: The good example of those few kings who turned to God and tried to turn all the people back to God. As you read, ask God to help you not to turn away from Him, as the evil kings did.

★ **KEY VERSE**: *"If my people, who are called by my name, will humble themselves and pray and seek my face and turn from their wicked ways, then will I hear from heaven and will forgive their sin and will heal their land"* (7:14).

■ **Background**: From David to Jerusalem's fall was about 400 years.

"It is impossible to rightly govern the world without God and the Bible." —President George Washington

---

● **What's BIG in This Book**: God's people *return to Jerusalem* from captivity in Babylon, and they *rebuild the Temple*. They had come back to a city in ruins.

➤ **What to Look For**: Ezra's humble praying. As you read, think about the example of this brave hero who was humble before God, and obeyed God all his life. Notice also how difficult it was to complete the work of rebuilding God's Temple. When we are doing God's will, we often face great opposition.

★ **KEY VERSE**: *"The Lord our God has been kind to us. He has let some of us come back from captivity. He has let us live in safety in his holy place. And so our God gives us hope and a little relief from our captivity"* (9:8).

■ **Background**: Only a very small number of God's people returned to the Promised Land. The Bible calls them "a remnant" (9:8,14-15).

My inner robe and coat were torn. And I fell on my knees with my hands spread out to the Lord my God. I prayed, "My God, I am too ashamed and embarrassed to lift up my face to you. I am in disgrace because our sins are so many they are higher than our heads."

—EZRA 9:5-6

It was night....I was inspecting the walls of Jerusalem. They had been broken down. And the gates had been destroyed by fire.... Finally I turned and went back in through the Valley Gate.
—NEHEMIAH 2:13-15

Nehemiah

● **What's BIG in This Book:** The *rebuilding of Jerusalem's walls,* and Nehemiah's strong leadership.

➤ **What to Look For:** How Nehemiah put his plan into action. Nehemiah was a leader who knew how to take charge and get things done. But more importantly, he was a man of prayer (like Ezra) who knew what *God* wanted him to do. Notice also how Nehemiah responded to the enemies who tried to stop him.

★ **KEY VERSE:** *"So the wall of Jerusalem was completed.... It took 52 days to rebuild. Then all our enemies heard about it.... They understood that the work had been done with the help of our God"* (6:15-16).

■ **Background:** Nehemiah's name means "comforted by God." Before he went to Jerusalem, he was an important officer in the court of the king of Persia.

> *"When you have read the Bible, you will know it is the word of God, because you will have found it the key to your own heart, your own happiness and your own duty."* — President Woodrow Wilson

● **What's BIG in This Book:** The *bravery* of Queen Esther as she went about saving her family and all the Jews in Persia from being killed.

Esther

➤ **What to Look For:** How God takes care of His people. God's name isn't mentioned in this book…but as you read it carefully, you'll see Him in control over all the exciting events of this story.

★ **KEY VERSE:** *"Mordecai gave orders to say to Esther: 'Just because you live in the king's palace, don't think that out of all the Jews you alone will escape. You might keep quiet at this time…. But you and your father's family will all die. And who knows, you may have been chosen queen for just such a time as this'"* (4:13-14).

■ **Background:** The story of Esther actually took place *before* the events described in the book of Nehemiah.

In the TORAH and HISTORY books, we see the full Old Testament story —the events from beginning to end.

Now, in the POETRY & WISDOM books and in the PROPHETS, we go back to that story to see what God's people were thinking and feeling as these events took place.

WISDOM & POETRY

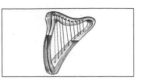

Job ● <u>**What's BIG in This Book**</u>: How *God is in control* even when bad things happen to good people.

➤ <u>**What to Look For**</u>: God's words sounding out to Job in a storm. From an attack by Satan, Job had lost his wealth, his children, and his health. But he did not lose his trust in God, so God spoke to him. As you read this book, ask yourself, How would I respond if I lost most of my family, and became very poor and very sick? Would I still trust in God? Would I listen to what He had to tell me?

★ <u>**KEY VERSE**</u>: *"God knows the way that I take. When he has tested me, I will come out pure as gold"* (23:10).

■ <u>**Background**</u>: The advice given by Job's three friends takes up much of the book. They said that when bad things happen to us, it's always because of our sin. But God said these three men were wrong.

"Job…are you the one that commands the eagle to fly and build his nest so high? The eagle lives on a high cliff and stays there at night. The rocky peak is his protected place. From there he looks for his food. His eyes can see it from far away. His young eat blood. And where there is something dead, the eagle is there.
—JOB 39:27-30

● **What's BIG in This Book:** *The honest sharing of our feelings with God, and His clear answers to us.*

➤ **What to Look For:** New ways to: •praise God *(for example, see Psalms 40, 98 or 144)...* •pray for your own needs *(6, 25 or 61)*, and for other people *(67, 122)...* •worship God *(24, 63)...* •give thanks to God *(100, 136)...*•understand what God is like *(86, 146)...* •understand God's care for you *(103, 145)...* •understand who you really are *(8, 139)...* •understand Jesus Christ *(2, 22)...* •understand God's Word *(19, 119)...* •understand how God wants you to live *(15, 24).*

Look also for: •Forgiveness for your sins *(32, 51 or 130)...* •comfort when you're hurting *(16, 23)...* •strength when you're fearful *(46, 121)...* •encouragement when others persecute you *(123, 143)...* •peace when you're upset *(4, 131)...* •wisdom for living a good life *(1, 90).*

★ **KEY VERSE:** *"Lord, hear me when I call. Be kind and answer me. My heart said of you, 'Go, worship him.' So I come to worship you, Lord"* (27:7-8).

■ **Background:** The word *psalm* means "song." Our book of Psalms is a collection of five numbered songbooks. Each songbook goes along with one of the five books of the Torah: Genesis goes with Book 1 *(Psalms 1-41);* Exodus with Book 2 *(Psalms 42-72);* Leviticus with Book 3 *(Psalms 73-89);* Numbers with Book 4 *(Psalms 90-106);* and Deuteronomy with Book 5 *(Psalms 107-150).*

In most English songs and poetry, words rhyme according to sound:	But Hebrew poetry (as in the Psalms) matches thought with thought. The *ideas* repeat, instead of the sounds:
Roses are red, *violets are blue,* *God's Word is sweet,* *and God's Word is true.*	*Lord, every morning you hear my voice.* *Every morning I tell you what I need.* *(Psalm 5:3)*

The right word spoken at the right time is as beautiful as gold apples in a silver bowl.

—PROVERBS 25:11

Proverbs

● <u>**What's BIG in This Book**</u>: *Wisdom,* which begins with having reverence and respect for God.

➤ <u>**What to Look For**</u>: Nuggets of wisdom to help you live in a way that fits with how God made the world. The wisdom taught in Proverbs has been built-in to this world by God. We can't find lasting happiness if we keep going against it. As you read, ask yourself how the truth of Proverbs compares with the way you live.

★ <u>**KEY VERSE**</u>: The words spoken by Wisdom in 8:33-35—*"Listen to my teaching, and you will be wise. Do not ignore it. Those who listen to me are happy. They stand watching at my door every day. They are at my open doorway, wanting to be with me. Whoever finds me finds life."*

■ <u>**Background**</u>: Just as David was the chief writer of the Psalms, so his son Solomon was the chief writer of the Proverbs.

- **What's BIG in This Book**: The *emptiness* of trying to find lasting happiness in anything besides God.

Ecclesiastes

➤ **What to Look For**: All the different things that will *not* give us lasting happiness. The fun things of this life cannot give us fun forever. Only honoring God and obeying Him will give us lasting pleasure and peace. Solomon, who wrote this book, got away from God and tried everything else. But he learned his lesson. And he passes it on to us so *we* don't have to learn this truth the hard way.

★ **KEY VERSE**: *"I know anything God does will continue forever. People cannot add anything to what God has done. And they cannot take anything away from it. God does it this way to cause people to honor him"* (3:14).

■ **Background**: In this book Solomon says that all things here on earth are like a vapor or breath. They do not last.

- **What's BIG in This Book**: *Love between husband and wife.* This is a book of heav-

Song of Solomon

enly love—both because the love between husband and wife is pleasing to God in heaven, and also because this love is a picture of the love Jesus Christ has for *His* bride. And who is His bride? The New Testament tells us that the Bride of Christ is the Church—*US!*

➤ **What to Look For**: The words that say how much the husband and wife enjoy each other.

★ **KEY VERSE**: *"I belong to my lover. And my lover belongs to me"* (6:3).

■ **Background**: This book is also called Canticles, or the Song of Songs.

"MAJOR" PROPHETS

Isaiah

● <u>**What's BIG in This Book**</u>: *The promise of Messiah,* the Servant of the Lord, the Prince of Peace: Jesus!

➤ <u>**What to Look For**</u>: What Isaiah tells us about God, what he tells us about Messiah or Christ (who would be born 700 years later), and what he tells us about the future when the Lord comes back to the earth. God gave Isaiah a glorious view of all of these.

★ <u>**KEY VERSE**</u>: *"A child will be born to us. God will give a son to us. He will be responsible for leading the people. His name will be Wonderful Counselor, Powerful God, Father Who Lives Forever, Prince of Peace"* (9:6).

■ <u>**Background**</u>: Isaiah's name means "the salvation of the LORD." His book has the same number of chapters as the Bible has books—66. Isaiah's last chapter ends in the same way the Bible's last book does: by describing a new heaven and a new earth.

Jeremiah

● <u>**What's BIG in This Book**</u>: The *disaster* about to come upon God's people, as His punishment for their sin. Jeremiah sounded the warning, but they did not listen.

➤ <u>**What to Look For**</u>: How God gave His people plenty of opportunities to turn away from their sin, and to turn back to Him.

★ <u>**KEY VERSE**</u>: *"Your evil will bring punishment to you. The wrong you have done will teach you a lesson. Think about it and understand. It is a terrible evil to turn away from the Lord your God"* (2:19).

■ <u>**Background**</u>: Jeremiah was the only man in the Bible who was told not to marry (16:2). Jeremiah was a prophet during the reigns of the last five kings of Judah—the southern kingdom of God's people —before the Babylonians destroyed Jerusalem and carried the people away into captivity.

In that day men will throw away to the rodents and bats their idols of silver and idols of gold, which they made to worship. They will flee to caverns in the rocks.

—ISAIAH 2:20-21

● **What's BIG in This Book:** *Tears of sorrow* for the horrible judgment that came to Jerusalem.

Lamentations

By including this book in the Bible, God tells us clearly that He does not enjoy having to punish His people.

➤ **What to Look For:** How much this sorrow hurts. Great sorrow comes from great love. God's love for His people was great. As you read, ask yourself how much sorrow you feel for the wrong things which people around you do, and the way their sin hurts them.

★ **KEY VERSE:** *"My eyes are weak from crying. I am troubled. I feel as if I have been poured out on the ground because my people have been destroyed"* (2:11).

■ **Background:** This book was written by the prophet Jeremiah, whose heart was broken.

THE OLD TESTAMENT, Book by Book ••• *371*

Ezekiel

● <u>**What's BIG in This Book**</u>: *Punishment from God,* followed by *forgiveness and healing from God.*

➤ <u>**What to Look For**</u>: Ezekiel's vision of the Lord, a vision of fire and glory. Notice also how black Ezekiel saw the sin of God's people, and how bright their future when God healed and restored them.

★ <u>**KEY VERSE**</u>: *"I will put a new way to think inside you. I will take out the stubborn heart like stone from your bodies. And I will give you an obedient heart of flesh. I will put my Spirit inside you"* (36:26-27).

■ <u>**Background**</u>: Ezekiel prophesied to God's people in captivity in Babylon, where he had been taken when he was twenty years old. Ezekiel's name means "God strengthens me." Ezekiel "acted out" many of the messages which God gave him for the people. He preached in the streets of Babylon.

King Darius was very happy. He told his servants to lift Daniel out of the lions' den. So they lifted him out and did not find any injury on him. This was because Daniel had trusted in his God.

—DANIEL 6:23

Daniel

● **What's BIG in This Book**: *God's plans for the future.*

➤ **What to Look For**: What Daniel was like as a man. What made him so brave and strong? Look also at the amazing dreams in this book.

★ **KEY VERSE**: *"God gives wisdom to people so they become wise. And he helps people learn and know things. He makes known secrets that are deep and hidden. He knows what is hidden in darkness, and light lives with him"* (2:21-22).

■ **Background**: Daniel's name means "God is my Judge." His book is considered a key to the prophecy in all the Scriptures. He speaks of times and dates in the future when God will accomplish His plans for all the world—not just for God's people.

> The Prophets—the last part of the Old Testament before we begin the New Testament—tell us more about Jesus Christ than any of the books that have gone before. The growing rose bud is almost ready to open in full bloom!

"MINOR" PROPHETS

Hosea

● **What's BIG in This Book**: *God's faithful love for His people, despite their sin.*

➤ **What to Look For**: The hope which God still holds out to those who have not been faithful to Him.

★ **KEY VERSE**: *"Come, let's go back to the Lord. He has hurt us, but he will heal us. He has wounded us, but he will bandage our wounds. In a short while he will put new life in us. We will not have to wait long for him to raise us up. Then we may live in his presence"* (6:1-2).

■ **Background**: Hosea's name means "salvation." God commanded Hosea to marry a woman who did not really love him, and would not be faithful to him. This was a picture of the way that God's people were being unfaithful to the Lord.

Joel

● **What's BIG in This Book**: *The day of God's judgment,* followed by a time of blessing.

➤ **What to Look For**: Both the "hard" side of God's dealings with His people, and the "soft" side: His punishment and His goodness. Joel speaks of "the day of the Lord," when God judges all sin. He also speaks of a day when a plague of locusts would cover the land and eat up all the food. This was a picture of what the day of God's judgment would be.

★ **KEY VERSE**: *"Let your heart be broken. Come back to the Lord your God. He is kind and shows mercy. He doesn't become angry quickly. He has great love. He would rather forgive than punish"* (2:13).

■ **Background**: Joel's name means "The LORD is my God."

Come, let's go back to the Lord. He has hurt us, but he will heal us. He has wounded us, but he will bandage our wounds. In a short while he will put new life in us.... Let's learn about the Lord. Let's try hard to know who he is.

—HOSEA 6:1-3

● **What's BIG in This Book**: *Sin must bring punishment.* Why? Because God is a God of justice.

Amos

➤ **What to Look For:** The reasons God sends His judgment. Amos announced the Lord's judgment upon both God's people and their neighbors. Notice the sins which Amos singles out.

★ **KEY VERSE:** *"Let justice flow like a river. Let goodness flow like a stream that never stops"* (5:24).

■ **Background**: Amos was a farmer. His name means "burdened." He said, *"I do not make my living as a prophet.... I make my living as a shepherd. And I take care of sycamore trees. But the Lord took me away from tending the sheep. He said to me, 'Go, prophesy to my people...'"* (7:14-15).

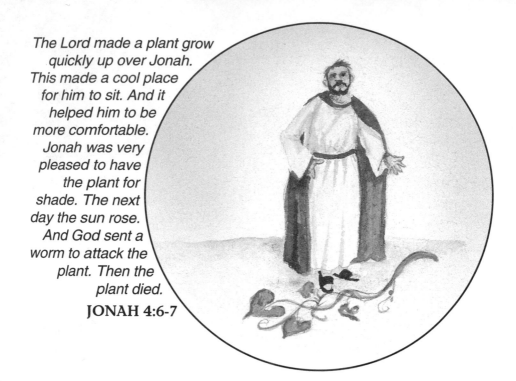

The Lord made a plant grow quickly up over Jonah. This made a cool place for him to sit. And it helped him to be more comfortable. Jonah was very pleased to have the plant for shade. The next day the sun rose. And God sent a worm to attack the plant. Then the plant died.

JONAH 4:6-7

Obadiah

● <u>**What's BIG in This Book**</u>: *Judgment* upon a proud and ungodly nation.

➤ <u>**What to Look For**</u>: God's view of human pride. The nation of Edom was a proud enemy to God's people, and Edom was glad when Babylon took Israel captive. So through Obadiah, God showed that Edom was doomed.

★ <u>**KEY VERSE**</u>: *"The people of Jacob, the Israelites, will be like a fire. And the people of Joseph will be like a flame. But the people of Esau, the Edomites, will be like dry stalks. The people of Jacob will set these stalks on fire. They will burn up the Edomites"* (verse 18).

■ <u>**Background**</u>: Obadiah's name means "Servant." This book is the shortest in the Old Testament.

● **What's BIG in This Book:** *God cares for EVERYONE.*

➤ **What to Look For:** How God shows His mercy to all.
Jonah didn't want to take God's warning to the city of Nineveh, because he was afraid the people there would believe God's Word, and turn from their sin. And that's exactly what happened! Jonah wanted God to destroy Nineveh, but God did not.

★ **KEY VERSE:** *"Surely I can show concern for the great city Nineveh. There are many animals in that city. And there are more than 120,000 people living there. Those people simply do not know right from wrong!"* (4:11).

■ **Background:** Jonah's name means "Dove." Unlike the other books in the Major and Minor Prophets, the book of Jonah is a story about the prophet, rather than a collection of his prophecies.

Jonah

● **What's BIG in This Book:** *The coming King,* to be born in Bethlehem. He would be a king of justice, and God will judge all those who cheat and do wrong.

➤ **What to Look For:** How God hates sin, and yet loves sinners. Look for the full picture of God that Micah gives. What is His hatred like? What is His love like? And look for the sins that God condemns through Micah. This is also the book that gives the prophecy of Christ being born in Bethlehem—*"one of the smallest towns in Judah"* (5:2).

★ **KEY VERSE:** *"The Lord has told you what is good. He has told you what he wants from you: Do what is right to other people. Love being kind to others. And live humbly, trusting your God"* (6:8).

■ **Background:** Micah's name means "Who is like the LORD?"

Micah

The Lord God gives me my strength. He makes me like a deer, which does not stumble. He leads me safely on the steep mountains.

—HABAKKUK 3:19

Nahum

● **What's BIG in This Book**: *God's punishment for a wicked city.*

➤ **What to Look For:** The awesome, fiery power of God's judgment upon wickedness. One hundred years after the great city of Nineveh turned away from sin because of the preaching of Jonah, the prophet Nahum gave this message of judgment. Nineveh was the capital city of Assyria, the most powerful nation on earth.

★ **KEY VERSE:** *"The Lord is good. He gives protection in times of trouble. He knows who trusts in him. But he will completely destroy the city of Nineveh"* (1:7-8).

■ **Background**: Nahum's name means "Comforter."

● **What's BIG in This Book**: *God's victory and* **Habakkuk**
salvation for the people who believe in Him.

➤ **What to Look For**: The prayers of Habakkuk in this book, and the answers he received from God. Habakkuk saw the way a terrible enemy would attack God's people, and he wanted to know why. He had struggles and doubts, so he took his questions to the Lord. Do you take *your* questions to the Lord?

★ **KEY VERSE**: *"See, the nation that is evil and trusts in itself will fail. But those who do right because they trust in God will live"* (2:4).

■ **Background**: Habakkuk's name means "Embrace." Habakkuk spoke on the people's behalf to God, and he spoke on God's behalf to the people.

"The longer you read the Bible, the more you will like it; it will grow sweeter and sweeter." —English Bible teacher William Romaine

---

● **What's BIG in This Book**: *Blessings for the people* **Zephaniah**
who are rescued by the Lord.

➤ **What to Look For**: How God's punishment and His love are connected. The first part of this book is a message of judgment: *"The Lord's day of judging is coming soon…. The cry will be very sad on that day. Even soldiers will cry…. It will be a day of destruction and ruin. It will be a day of darkness and gloom. It will be a day of clouds and blackness"* (1:14-15). Then comes a message of hope: *"Sing, Jerusalem. Israel, shout for joy! Jerusalem, be happy. Rejoice with all your heart. The Lord has stopped punishing you. He has sent your enemies away"* (3:14-15).

★ **KEY VERSE**: *"The Lord will be happy with you. You will rest in his love. He will sing and be joyful about you"* (3:17).

■ **Background**: Zephaniah's name means "Hidden by the LORD."

Haggai

● __What's BIG in This Book__: *A new Temple of God.*

➤ __What to Look For:__ How God's people responded to the message Haggai gave them about building God's house. How was this different from the way the people responded to the preaching of Jeremiah many years before?

★ __KEY VERSE:__ *"This is what the Lord of heaven's armies says: 'Think about what you have done. Go up to the mountains. Bring back wood and build the Temple. Then I will be pleased with it and be honored,' says the Lord"* (1:7-8).

■ __Background:__ Haggai's name means "Festival." He was the first of three prophets (the other two are Zechariah and Malachi) who spoke at about the same time to the small "remnant" of God's people who returned to Jerusalem and Judah after the captivity in Babylon.

Zechariah

● __What's BIG in This Book:__ *The Lord remembers His people.* He will send them Messiah, their Priest and King.

➤ __What to Look For:__ The many visions Zechariah had. These are filled with powerful pictures, and they tell of the coming Messiah. Notice also the encouragement Zechariah gave the people for rebuilding the Temple, just as Haggai did.

★ __KEY VERSE:__ *"Rejoice, people of Jerusalem. Shout for joy, people of Jerusalem. Your king is coming to you. He does what is right, and he saves. He is gentle and riding on a donkey. He is on the colt of a donkey"* (9:9).

■ __Background:__ Zechariah's name means "One whom the LORD remembers."

● **What's BIG in This Book**: A last warning to God's | **Malachi**

people: *Judgment is coming!*

➤ **What to Look For**: The sins of God's people which Malachi called attention to. God's people had been brought back from captivity, but now in the Promised Land they were deep in sin again. Malachi warns them of God's punishment.

★ **KEY VERSE**: *"There is a day coming that will be like a hot furnace. All the proud and evil people will be like straw. On that day they will be completely burned up. Not a root or branch will be left,' says the Lord....'But for you who honor me, goodness will shine on you like the sun. There will be healing in its rays. You will jump around, like calves freed from their stalls'"* (4:1-2).

■ **Background**: Malachi's name means "Messenger of the LORD."

The names of those who honored the Lord and respected him were written in a scroll. The Lord will remember them. The Lord says, "They belong to me."

—MALACHI 3:16

400 Years of Silence...

Between Old Testament and New Testament

After the last Old Testament books were written, another 400 years would pass before the coming of Christ. These four centuries are sometimes called the "400 Silent Years," because God's Spirit did not cause any more books to be added to the Scriptures until after Jesus Christ came.

During these 400 years, the Greek language (the language in which the New Testament was first written) became the most important language in the world. And the Roman Empire took control over almost every other nation for many hundreds of miles in every direction. By the time Jesus was born, the land of Israel was much different from the nation which David and Isaiah and Malachi had known. Two of the biggest differences were the sound of the Greek language everywhere, and the sight of Roman soldiers throughout the land.

Jesus brought out the true meaning of everything that had gone before in the Bible. In His hometown of Nazareth, Jesus read aloud to the people from the Prophets. Then He said, *"Today this Scripture is fulfilled in your hearing."*

In His great Sermon on the Mount, Jesus said, *"Do not think that I have come to abolish (or destroy) the Law or the Prophets; I have not come to abolish them but to fulfill them."*

The Old Testament is like a river channel that someone dug out, waiting for the water to flow through it. When Jesus came, He was like the rushing stream that followed the course of the channel, and filled up that riverbed!

SUPER TRUTH
in the Bible

In Revelation, Jesus says, "I am…the ***beginning*** and the ***end.***"

The New Testament begins and ends with Jesus Christ.
The same is true for all the Bible. It begins and ends
with Jesus Christ.

This also is true in my life and your life.
Jesus is our *Starting Point,* and Jesus is our *Finish Line.*
He gave us life to begin with; and when our life on this earth
is over, we will stand before Him to hear what He has to say
about the way we lived.

When we want to understand something better,
usually it helps to go back to the beginning.
This is true in understanding the Bible better, too.
It's best to go back to the beginning…
and that Beginning is Jesus.

Since the Gospels at the start of the New Testament are where
we find the fullest and clearest story of Jesus, the Gospels
make an excellent place to start reading your Bible.

But don't stop there, because you'll find Jesus everywhere
in the Bible. And the more you get to know Him,
the more you'll want to know Him better.

GOSPELS

A man was there with a crippled hand. Some Jews there were looking for a reason to accuse Jesus of doing wrong. So they asked him, "Is it right to heal on the Sabbath day?"

Jesus answered, "If any of you has a sheep, and it falls into a ditch on the Sabbath day, then you will take the sheep and help it out of the ditch. Surely a man is more important than a sheep.... Then Jesus said to the man with the crippled hand, "Let me see your hand." The man put his hand out, and the hand became well again, the same as the other hand.

—MATTHEW 12:10-13

● **What's BIG in This Book:** *Jesus Christ the King,* the Son of David, and the promised Messiah, as prophesied in the Old Testament.

➤ **What to Look For:** Christ's teachings about the kingdom of God. Have you made Jesus your King? What does that mean to you?

★ **KEY VERSE:** *"Don't think that I have come to destroy the law of Moses or the teaching of the prophets. I have not come to destroy their teachings but to do what they said"* (5:17).

■ **Background:** The apostle Matthew wrote this book for his fellow Jews. Of the four Gospels, Matthew alone includes the account of the wise men coming to see baby Jesus, the miracle of the fish with the coin in its mouth, many of the parables, and many of Jesus' teachings, such as these: *"Come to me, all of you who are tired and have heavy loads. I will give you rest"* (11:28); and *"Go and make followers of all people in the world.... You can be sure that I will be with you always. I will continue with you until the end of the world"* (28:19-20).

● **What's BIG in This Book:** *Jesus Christ, the obedient Servant of the Lord,* and the Servant of all people.

➤ **What to Look For:** The wonderful works of Christ. In Mark we see more miracles of Jesus than teachings of Jesus. Jesus is a Man of action and power. If you have decided to follow Jesus, are you ready for a life of action and power?

★ **KEY VERSE:** *"The Son of Man did not come to be served. He came to serve. The Son of Man came to give his life to save many people"* (10:45).

■ **Background:** John Mark wrote this book, which is the shortest and fastest-moving of the four gospels. Mark was not one of the twelve disciples, but he traveled with the apostle Paul on his first missionary trip, and he was also a friend of the apostle Peter. His book may well have been the first of the four gospels to be written.

Luke • **What's BIG in This Book:** *Jesus Christ the Son of Man, the Perfect Man, and the Savior of all mankind.*

➤ **What to Look For:** The parables of Christ, the compassion of Christ, and His friendship and concern for people of all kinds. Look also for the Holy Spirit's part in Jesus' ministry. By the power of the Holy Spirit in *your* life, are you learning to see other people with the compassion which Jesus had?

★ **KEY VERSE:** *"The Son of Man came to find lost people and save them"* (19:10).

■ **Background:** Luke, a doctor and friend of the apostle Paul, wrote this book for people who were not Jews. His gospel tells us the most about Jesus' birth and childhood, such as the account of the shepherds and angels in Bethlehem, and Jesus' visit to the Temple in Jerusalem at age twelve. And only Luke tells us about Zacchaeus, the visit in Mary and Martha's home when Martha was busy, and the stories of the Good Samaritan, the lost coin, and the prodigal son.

Some Old Testament Prophecies Fulfilled in Christ

Born in Bethlehem (Micah 5:2, Matthew 2:6)
Born of a virgin (Isaiah 7:14, Luke 1:26-35)
John the Baptist preparing the way (Isaiah 40:3, Malachi 4:5,
    Mark 1:2-4, 9:11-13)
Anointed by the Spirit (Isaiah 11:1-2, Mark 1:9-11)
Ministry in Galilee (Isaiah 9:1-2, Matthew 4:12-17)
Riding into Jerusalem on a donkey (Zechariah 9:9, Mark 12:10)
Betrayed by a Friend (Psalm 41:9, Matthew 26:47-50)
His disciples leave Him (Zechariah 13:7, Matthew 26:31)
False witness against Him (Psalm 35:11, Matthew 26:59-60)
Silent before His accusers (Psalm 38:13, Isaiah 53:7, Mark 15:1-6)

● **What's BIG in This Book:** *Jesus Christ the Son of God.*

➤ **What to Look For:** The conversations Christ had with others. Look for all the many reasons to believe in Christ, and for how Jesus is the Way and the Truth and the Life. Do you believe Jesus is the Son of God? If so, why do you believe it?

★ **KEY VERSE:** *"Jesus did many other miracles before his followers that are not written in this book. But these are written so that you can believe that Jesus is the Christ, the Son of God. Then, by believing, you can have life through his name"* (20:30-31).

■ **Background:** The apostle John wrote this book to help people believe in Jesus. It is the most different of the four gospels. Only John tells us about Jesus turning water into wine, His talk one night with Nicodemus, His visit with the woman at the well of Samaria, His raising of Lazarus from the dead, His healing of the man born blind, and His words about being the good shepherd, the light of the world, the bread of life, the vine, and much more.

Scorned, disgraced, and shamed (Psalm 69:19, Mark 15:16-20)
Crucified, His hands and feet pierced (Psalm 22:16, Mark 15:22-24)
Crucified between two robbers (Isaiah 53:12, Luke 23:32)
Wounded for our sins (Isaiah 53:5-10, Romans 4:25)
His willingness to die (Psalm 40:6-8, John 12:27-33)
Lots cast for His clothing (Psalm 22:18, John 19:23-24)
Mocked on the cross by the crowds (Psalm 22:7-8, Luke 23:35-38)
Prayer for His enemies (Isaiah 53:12, Psalm 109:4, Luke 23:34)
Darkness at the crucifixion (Amos 8:9, Matthew 27:45)
Forsaken by God (Psalm 22:1, Matthew 27:46)
Given vinegar to drink (Psalm 69:21, John 19:28-29)
His side pierced (Zechariah 12:10, John 19:34-37)
Raised up from the dead (Psalm 16:10, Luke 24:1-6)

Then the big waves began to break the back of the ship to pieces.... Julius, the officer, ordered everyone who could swim to jump into the water and swim to land. The rest used wooden boards or pieces of the ship.

—ACTS 27:41-44

ACTS

Acts

● **What's BIG in This Book:** The church is born, and receives power from the Holy Spirit; *the gospel of Christ spreads out to all the world.*

➤ **What to Look For:** Why the first Christians were so bold and brave; why they shared everything with one another; how the Holy Spirit sent Christians out in every direction to share the good news of Jesus Christ. All the action that began in Acts is still going on today; what part do you want to have in it?

★ **KEY VERSE:** *"But the Holy Spirit will come to you. Then you will receive power. You will be my witnesses—in Jerusalem, in all of Judea, in Samaria, and in every part of the world"* (1:8).

■ **Background:** Acts was written by Luke, and it's a companion book to his gospel.

LETTERS BY PAUL

Romans

● **What's BIG in This Book:** *The true meaning of the gospel;* how we find peace with God.

➤ **What to Look For:** A clear and careful explanation of how God saved us from our sin; how God makes us right; how God makes us dead to sin but alive in Jesus Christ; the meaning of faith; how we can know the Holy Spirit; how God shows His mercy to all; how we can worship God in the right way—that is, by the way we live!

★ **KEY VERSE:** *"All people have sinned and are not good enough for God's glory. People are made right with God by his grace, which is a free gift. They are made right with God by being made free from sin through Jesus Christ"* (3:23-24).

■ **Background:** Paul wrote this letter to Christians in Rome, whom he hoped to be visiting soon.

How often do you get mail? God's Word is like a personal letter to us, from the most important Person in the universe—the One who loves you more than anyone else does, and who was willing to die for you to prove His love.

Just think! If you always read the Bible every day, you'll get a letter from Him every day for the rest of your life!

1 Corinthians

● **What's BIG in This Book**: *Living by the Spirit of God.*

➤ **What to Look For**: How to solve the problems that come up in churches today, and how to get along with one another; what wisdom really is; how to be free in Christ from things that enslave us; how to take communion, the Lord's Supper; the gifts given to us by the Holy Spirit; why love is always best; what the gospel is; how we will take part in the resurrection of Jesus Christ; and what our bodies will be like in heaven.

★ **KEY VERSE**: *"Love patiently accepts all things. It always trusts, always hopes, and always continues strong. Love never ends"* (13:7-8).

■ **Background**: Paul was writing to a church which he himself had started in Corinth, a city in Greece.

2 Corinthians

● **What's BIG in This Book**: *The great privilege of being one of God's workers;* serving others with the gospel of Christ.

➤ **What to Look For**: How to forgive others who have done great wrong; how to live a life of victory in Christ; why we share the gospel with people who don't believe in Jesus; how we live by faith, and become friends with God; why we should be careful in what we do with unbelievers; the happiness of giving money to help God's people; the hard lessons Paul learned in his life.

★ **KEY VERSE**: *"Thanks be to God, who always leads us in victory through Christ. God uses us to spread his knowledge everywhere like a sweet-smelling perfume"* (2:14).

■ **Background**: Paul uses this letter to defend his work as an apostle.

Even Satan changes himself to look like an angel of light. So it does not surprise us if Satan's servants also make themselves look like servants who work for what is right. But in the end they will be punished for the things they do.

—2 CORINTHIANS 11:14-15

Galatians

● **What's BIG in This Book:** *Our freedom in Christ; our gospel is the gospel of grace.*

➤ **What to Look For:** Why there is only one gospel; a disagreement between Peter and Paul, and how it was worked out; why we must live by faith, and not by keeping rules; how to live by the Holy Spirit, and enjoy good things because of it.

★ **KEY VERSE:** *"God called you to be free. But do not use your freedom as an excuse to do the things that please your sinful self. Serve each other with love. The whole law is made complete in this one command: 'Love your neighbor as you love yourself'"* (5:13-14).

■ **Background:** In this letter, Paul called his readers "foolish Galatians" because they were living by rules instead of living in the freedom we have in Jesus Christ.

Ephesians

● **What's BIG in This Book**: *Our riches in Christ; in Jesus Christ we are all part of one Church.*

➤ **What to Look For**: Our blessings in heaven and on earth that come to us in Christ; how we have gone from death to life; why all Christians are brothers and sisters; how we should live since we're all part of the same family; how to live as a child of light; why we must put on God's armor.

★ **KEY VERSE**: *"In Christ we were chosen to be God's people. God had already chosen us to be his people, because that is what he wanted. And God is the One who makes everything agree with what he decides and wants"* (1:11).

■ **Background**: Paul was a prisoner in Rome when he wrote this letter.

Philippians

● **What's BIG in This Book**: *The joy of knowing Christ,* even when we face hardships.

➤ **What to Look For**: How Paul's hardships led to good things; how to be unselfish like Jesus was, and serve one another with joy; the great joy and privilege of knowing Christ, sharing in both His death and His life; why we can always be joyful.

★ **KEY VERSE**: *"Do not worry about anything. But pray and ask God for everything you need. And when you pray, always give thanks. And God's peace will keep your hearts and minds in Christ Jesus. The peace that God gives is so great that we cannot understand it"* (4:6-7).

■ **Background**: This letter also was written from a Roman prison. But Paul wasn't complaining. He was glad that the prison guards and others there now had an opportunity to hear about the gospel.

- **What's BIG in This Book**: How Jesus Christ is perfectly God, and our perfect Leader.

➤ **What to Look For**: Why it's so important to understand that Jesus is fully God; Paul's example of hard work in teaching God's people about Christ; why Christ is the right foundation for our lives; why we should follow Him, and not rules made up by other people; how we can keep our eyes on Christ in heaven even now.

★ **KEY VERSE**: *"As you received Christ Jesus the Lord, so continue to live in him. Keep your roots deep in him and have your lives built on him. Be strong in the faith, just as you were taught. And always be thankful"* (2:6–7).

■ **Background**: This is another letter from prison in Rome.

You were raised from death with Christ. So aim at what is in heaven, where Christ is sitting at the right hand of God. Think only about the things in heaven, not the things on earth.

—COLOSSIANS 3:1-2

You know that we treated each of you as a father treats his own children. We strengthened you, we comforted you, and we told you to live good lives for God. It is God who calls you to his glorious kingdom.

—1 THESSALONIANS 2:11-12

1 Thessalonians

● **What's BIG in This Book**: *Looking forward to the return of Jesus Christ.*

➤ **What to Look For:** The good example of the Thessalonian church; how Paul worked hard to help them, and now wants to see them again; how to live a life that pleases God; what we need to know about Jesus coming back to earth.

★ **KEY VERSE:** *"We pray that the Lord will make your love grow more and more for each other and for all people. We pray that you will love others as we love you and that your hearts will be made strong. Then you will be holy and without fault before our God and Father when our Lord Jesus comes with all his holy people"* (3:12).

■ **Background:** This was probably one of Paul's earliest letters to a church.

● **What's BIG in This Book**: *Finding comfort in the Lord as we wait for Him to come to earth again.*

➤ **What to Look For**: How God will someday send down fiery judgment on those who won't obey the gospel; the evil things that will happen in the world before Jesus comes back; how God loves us and has chosen us to be saved; the need to be a good worker.

★ **KEY VERSE**: *"We pray that the Lord Jesus Christ himself and God our Father will comfort you and strengthen you in every good thing you do and say. God loved us. Through his grace he gave us a good hope and comfort that continues forever"* (2:16-17).

■ **Background**: Paul wanted to clear up confusion among the Thessalonians about the return of Jesus Christ.

● **What's BIG in This Book**: *Taking care of God's people,* and not being harmed by false teachers.

➤ **What to Look For**: Paul's story about the mercy God showed to him; what to pray for our government leaders; the requirements for becoming a leader or a helper in God's Church; how to be a good servant to one another; how to treat older people and younger people; how to treat riches.

★ **KEY VERSE**: *"There is only one God. And there is only one way people can reach God. That way is through Jesus Christ, who is also a man. Jesus gave himself to pay for the sins of all people. Jesus is proof that God wants all people to be saved. And that proof came at the right time"* (2:5-6).

■ **Background**: Timothy was a young church leader, and a close friend of Paul's.

> "The Bible is all pure, all sincere; nothing too much;
> nothing wanting." —John Locke, English philosopher

2 Timothy

● **What's BIG in This Book**: *Being a good soldier of Jesus Christ.*

➤ **What to Look For**: Paul's brave encouragement for Timothy; why we should not be ashamed to tell people the gospel; how to be a good soldier, a winning athlete, or a wise farmer; Paul's thoughts about being in prison; how to please God in the way we serve Him and work for Him; the troubles that will come in the world in the last days; Paul's final words of hope as he expects to be put to death soon.

★ **KEY VERSE**: *"God did not give us a spirit that makes us afraid. He gave us a spirit of power and love and self-control"* (1:7).

■ **Background**: This letter is Paul's last one, and it, too, was written in prison; Paul said he knew he would soon be killed.

Titus

● **What's BIG in This Book**: *God's people are called to be good people.*

➤ **What to Look For**: God's requirements for leaders in His Church; the right things to teach older people and younger people; the right way for everyone to live; how God's kindness saved us from being foolish slaves to our bodies; why we are brand-new people now, washed in the Holy Spirit; the right things to teach in God's Church.

★ **KEY VERSE**: *"He gave himself for us; he died to free us from all evil. He died to make us pure people who belong only to him—people who are always wanting to do good things"* (2:14).

■ **Background**: Paul had sent Titus to be the leader of the churches on the island of Crete, and this letter told him how to do the job.

Teach younger women to love their husbands and children.

—**TITUS 2:4**

● **What's BIG in This Book:** *The story of a slave who became a Christian.*

Philemon

➤ **What to Look For:** Paul's kind and careful words to a man about accepting back a slave who once ran away—but who is coming back now as a Christian brother.

★ **KEY VERSE:** *"Onesimus was separated from you for a short time. Maybe that happened so that you could have him back forever—not to be a slave, but better than a slave, to be a loved brother. I love him very much. But you will love him even more. You will love him as a man and as a brother in the Lord"* (verses 15-16).

■ **Background:** This is another letter written by Paul from prison.

OTHER LETTERS

Hebrews

● **What's BIG in This Book:** *The many ways that Christ is so great.*

➤ **What to Look For:** Why Christ is greater than angels, and greater than Moses, and greater than the Old Testament way of offering sacrifices in the Temple; how Jesus is our High Priest now; how we can freely come close to God now because of what Jesus has done; how Christ took away our sins; the meaning of faith.

★ **KEY VERSE:** *"Let us look only to Jesus. He is the one who began our faith, and he makes our faith perfect. Jesus suffered death on the cross. But he accepted the shame of the cross as if it were nothing. He did this because of the joy that God put before him. And now he is sitting at the right side of God's throne"* (12:2).

■ **Background:** We do not know with certainty who wrote this letter.

James

● **What's BIG in This Book:** *Why our faith must be alive and working.*

➤ **What to Look For:** Why saying we have faith is not enough; why our faith must show itself in action; what to do when we need wisdom; the meaning of temptation; the true way to worship God; why we must control the things we say; why we sometimes get into arguments and fights; how to let God plan your life; why being rich is dangerous; why we need to be patient, and to keep praying.

★ **KEY VERSE:** *"If faith does nothing, then that faith is dead, because it is alone"* (2:17).

■ **Background:** This letter was probably written by James, the younger brother of Jesus. It may be the oldest of all the books in the New Testament.

Never think that some people are more important than others. Suppose someone comes into your church meeting wearing very nice clothes and a gold ring. At the same time a poor man comes in wearing old, dirty clothes. You show special attention to the one wearing nice clothes.... With evil thoughts you are deciding which person is better.

—JAMES 2:1-4

1 Peter

● **What's BIG in This Book:** Staying true to Christ when *suffering* comes our way.

➤ **What to Look For:** Why we must live holy lives; what price was paid for us so that we can live holy lives; how to grow stronger in our faith; how to follow Christ's example when we suffer something we don't deserve; how husbands and wives should live with one another; why we should expect to face suffering as we follow Jesus; how to use God's gifts wisely.

★ **KEY VERSE:** *"These troubles come to prove that your faith is pure. This purity of faith is worth more than gold. Gold can be proved to be pure by fire, but gold will ruin. But the purity of your faith will bring you praise and glory and honor when Jesus Christ comes again"* (1:7).

■ **Background:** The apostle Peter sent this letter to many churches.

2 Peter

● <u>**What's BIG in This Book**</u>: *Growing in the grace and power of the Lord.*

➤ <u>**What to Look For**</u>: Where to find all we need to live a good life; how to grow, step-by-step; hearing God's voice from heaven; guarding against false teachers; being certain that Jesus is coming again.

★ <u>**KEY VERSE**</u>: *"Jesus has the power of God. His power has given us everything we need to live and to serve God. We have these things because we know him. Jesus called us by his glory and goodness. Through his glory and goodness, he gave us the very great and rich gifts he promised us. With those gifts you can share in being like God. And so the world will not ruin you with its evil desires"* (1:3-4).

■ <u>**Background**</u>: Both of Peter's letters were written when there was much persecution against Christians.

It is good for you to follow closely what the prophets said. Their message is like a light shining in a dark place. That light shines until the day begins and the morning star rises in your hearts.

—2 PETER 1:19

> *"I have read the Bible through one hundred times, and always with increasing delight. Each time it seems like a new book to me."*
> —George Mueller, British man of faith

● **What's BIG in This Book**: *Living as God's children.*

> **What to Look For**: What it means to know God, and follow Christ; what God is like; how to know if we are following Christ or not; what it means to walk in the light of the truth; how to keep from sinning; how we can find forgiveness; what it means to be in love with the world instead of in love with the Lord; being on guard against the enemies of Christ; why we must love one another; where love comes from; how we can know for sure that we will go to heaven.

★ **KEY VERSE:** *"I write this letter to you who believe in the Son of God. I write so that you will know that you have eternal life now"* (5:13).

■ **Background:** John may have been the only apostle still alive when he wrote these three letters and the book of Revelation.

1 John

● **What's BIG in This Book**: Loving one another, and *staying away from false teachers.*

> **What to Look For**: How truth and love go together; John's happiness to hear that the people he taught about Christ were still following the truth; what love means; what to do about false teachers.

★ **KEY VERSE:** *"Loving means living the way he commanded us to live. And God's command is this: that you live a life of love. You have heard this command from the beginning"* (verse 6).

■ **Background:** In everything he wrote in the Bible, John had much to say about *truth* and *love*.

2 John

3 John

● **What's BIG in This Book**: *Helping Christian workers who teach God's truth.*

➤ **What to Look For**: More good news for John; why it is good to help Christian workers who travel around to teach God's truth; John's words about a man who lied.

★ **KEY VERSE**: *"My dear friend, it is good that you continue to help the brothers. You are helping those that you do not even know!"* (verse 5).

■ **Background**: The men whom John calls "the brothers" in this letter were Christian workers who traveled from church to church, teaching and preaching.

Jude

● **What's BIG in This Book**: *More warnings about false teachers;* staying true to our faith.

➤ **What to Look For**: Why we must fight for the faith; John's warning about secret enemies; remembering the examples of God's punishment; an argument between the devil and an angel; being sure of God's coming judgment against evil.

★ **KEY VERSE**: *"Dear friends, I wanted very much to write to you about the salvation we all share together. But I felt the need to write to you about something else: I want to encourage you to fight hard for the faith that God gave his holy people. God gave this faith once, and it is good for all time"* (verse 3).

■ **Background**: Jude was the brother of Jesus and of James.

REVELATION

● **What's BIG in This Book**: *Jesus Christ, our great King, returning to us in victory; a new heaven and a new earth; how to share in His victory now.*

➤ **What to Look For**: The sure victory of Jesus Christ over Satan and all evil; what Jesus wants everyone in our churches to know and do; how to stay faithful to Jesus while we wait for Him to come back; how God is worshiped in heaven; what heaven will be like for us.

★ **KEY VERSE**: *"Jesus is the One who says that these things are true. Now he says, 'Yes, I am coming soon.' Amen. Come, Lord Jesus!"* (22:20).

■ **Background**: This book is called "The Revelation of Jesus Christ." It was written by the apostle John when he was being kept on a small island, and saw and heard Jesus in a vision. It's an exciting book of hope, to keep us waiting faithfully for the time when Jesus will come back to us in a blaze of glory.

There was a woman who was clothed with the sun. The moon was under her feet. She had a crown of 12 stars on her head.... There was a giant red dragon.... He wanted to eat the woman's baby as soon as it was born.... But her child was taken up to God and to his throne.

—REVELATION
12:1-5

Soldiers from Assyria sometimes fought lions,
and sometimes fought Israel.

More Discoveries

Everyday Life in the Bible
Plants & Animals of the Bible
Weapons in the Bible
The Temple in Jerusalem
The Bible's Most Famous People
Miracles of Jesus
Parables of Jesus
Favorite Read-Aloud Passages
Bible Reading Calendar

Everyday Life in the Bible

A TENT HOME. "The Lord appeared to Abraham...while he was sitting at the entrance to his tent in the heat of the day" (Genesis 18:1).

A CAMEL CARAVAN. "The queen of Sheba arrived at Jerusalem with a very great caravan—with camels carrying spices, gold, and precious stones" (1 Kings 10:1-2).

A TYPICAL HOME IN ISRAEL. "The house of the righteous stands firm"
(Proverbs 12:7).

FISHERMEN. "When Jesus had finished speaking to the people, he said to Simon, 'Put out into deep water, and let down the nets for a catch.' Simon answered, 'Master, we've worked hard all night and haven't caught anything. But because you say so, I will let down the nets.' When they had done so, they caught such a large number of fish that their nets began to break" (Luke 5:1-6).

AT THE WELL. "A good person who gives in to evil is like a muddy spring or a dirty well" (Proverbs 25:26).

PLOWING A FIELD. "Jesus said, 'Anyone who begins to plow a field but keeps looking back is of no use in the kingdom of God'" (Luke 9:62).

A MARKETPLACE. "Jesus said to his disciples, 'Beware of the teachers of the law. They like to walk around in flowing robes and love to be greeted in the marketplaces...'" (Luke 20:46).

COINS. "Judas said, 'I will give Jesus to you. What will you pay me for doing this?' The priests gave Judas 30 silver coins" (Matthew 26:15).

EMPTY LAMPS. "At that time the kingdom of heaven will be like ten virgins who took their lamps and went out to meet the bridegroom. Five of them were foolish and five were wise. The foolish ones took their lamps but did not take any oil with them. The wise, however, took oil in jars along with their lamps" (Matthew 25:1-4).

TRAVELING BY FOOT AND BY DONKEY. "For a long time Israel was without the true God.... In those days no one could travel safely. There was much trouble in all the nations" (2 Chronicles 15:5).

MEN HAVING A MEAL. "If you sit down to eat with a ruler, notice the food that is in front of you. Control yourself if you have a big appetite. Don't be greedy for his fine foods. He might use that rich food to trick you" (Proverbs 23:1-3).

BAKING BREAD. "The Lord said to me.... 'Take wheat, barley, beans, small peas and millet seeds. And put them in one bowl. Make them into bread for yourself....'" (Ezekiel 4:9).

"Jesus said, 'My Father gives you the true bread from heaven. God's bread is the One who comes down from heaven and gives life to the world....I am the bread that gives life. He who comes to me will never be hungry. He who believes in me will never be thirsty'" (John 6:32-35).

LION CHASING A DEER. "If I hold up my head, you hunt me like a lion. And again you show your terrible power against me" (Job 10:16).

Plants & Animals in the Bible

CEDARS OF LEBANON. "The Lord's trees have plenty of water. They are the cedar trees of Lebanon, which he planted. The birds make their nests there" (Psalm 104:16-17).

GAZELLES. "Part of the people of Gad joined David at his protected place in the desert. They were brave warriors trained for war. They were skilled with shields and spears.... And they could run as fast as gazelles over the hills" (1 Chronicles 12:8).

GRAPES. "Then another angel came out of the temple in heaven. This angel also had a sharp sickle. And then another angel came from the altar. This angel has power over the fire. This angel called to the angel with the sharp sickle. He said, 'Take your sharp sickle and gather the bunches of grapes from the earth's vine. The earth's grapes are ripe'" (Revelation 14:17-18).

LOCUST. "John's clothes were made from camel's hair. He wore a leather belt around his waist. For food, he ate locusts and wild honey" (Matthew 3:4).

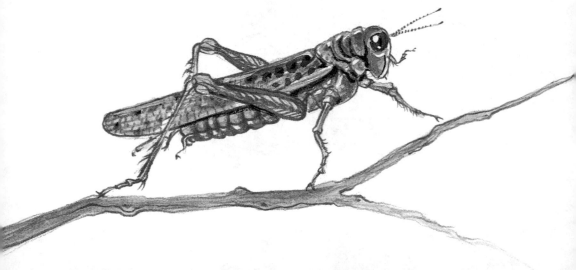

COBRA. "A new king will come.... Then a baby will be able to play near a cobra's hole. A child will be able to put his hand into the nest of a poisonous snake. They will not hurt or destroy each other on all my holy mountain. The earth will be full of the knowledge of the Lord, as the sea is full of water" Isaiah 11:1-9).

SCORPION. "The Lord your God led you through the vast and dreadful desert, that thirsty and waterless land, with its poisonous snakes and scorpions" (Deuteronomy 8:15).

Weapons in the Bible

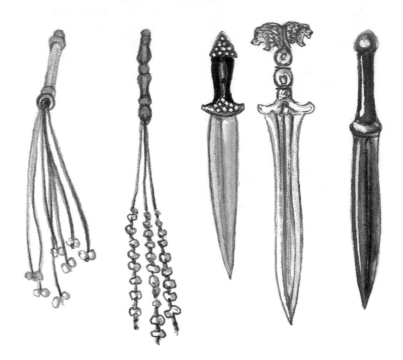

WHIPS AND SCOURGES. "When Pilate had scourged Jesus, he delivered him to be crucified" (Matthew 27:26).

KNIVES AND DAGGERS. "Each man grabbed his enemy's head. Then he stabbed his enemy's side with a knife. And the men fell down together" (2 Samuel 2:16).

SPEARS. "Although the Egyptian had a spear like a weaver's rod in his hand, Benaiah went against him with a club. He snatched the spear from the Egyptian's hand and killed him with his own spear" (1 Chronicles 11:23).

Tabernacle and Temple

THE TABERNACLE. "So all the work on the tabernacle, the Tent of Meeting, was completed. The Israelites did everything just as the Lord commanded Moses. Then they brought the tabernacle to Moses: the tent and all its furnishings....

"Moses inspected the work and saw that they had done it just as the Lord had commanded. So Moses blessed them.

"Then the Lord said to Moses: 'Set up the tabernacle, the Tent of Meeting, on the first day of the first month....' So the tabernacle was set up on the first day of the first month....

"Then the cloud covered the Tent of Meeting, and the glory of the Lord filled the tabernacle. Moses could not enter the Tent of Meeting because the cloud had settled upon it, and the glory of the Lord filled the tabernacle.

"In all the travels of the Israelites, whenever the cloud lifted from above the tabernacle, they would set out; but if the cloud did not lift, they did not set out—until the day it lifted. So the cloud of the Lord was over the tabernacle by day, and the fire was in the cloud by night, in the sight of all the house of Israel during all their travels."

(Exodus 39—40)

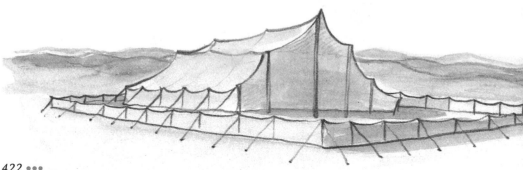

THE TEMPLE OF SOLOMON. "So Solomon began to build the Temple. This was 480 years after the people of Israel had left Egypt....

"The Lord spoke his word to Solomon: 'Obey all my laws and commands. If you do, I will do for you what I promised your father David. And I will live among the children of Israel in this Temple you are building. I will never leave the people of Israel.'

"So Solomon finished building the Temple.... It was finished exactly as it was planned. Solomon had worked seven years to build the Temple....

"Then King Solomon called for all the leaders of Israel to come to him in Jerusalem.... The priests put the Ark of the Covenant with the Lord in its right place. This was inside the Most Holy Place in the Temple....

"When the priests left the Holy Place, the cloud filled the Temple of the Lord. The priests could not continue their work. This was because the Temple was filled with the glory of the Lord."

(1 Kings 6—8)

The Bible's Most Famous People

READ ABOUT...

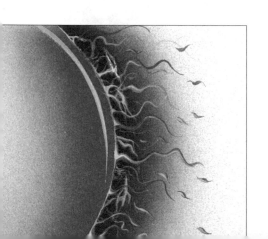

MOSES in the books of Exodus through Deuteronomy, and Hebrews 11:23-29

NAOMI in the book of Ruth

NATHAN in Second Samuel 7— First Kings 1

NEBUCHADNEZZAR in Second Kings 24—25, Second Chronicles 36, Jeremiah 39, and Daniel 2—4

NEHEMIAH in the book of Nehemiah

NICODEMUS in John 3, 7, 19

NOAH in Genesis 5:29—10:32 and Hebrews 11:7

PAUL (also called Saul) in Acts 8—9, 11, 13—28; and in his epistles (Romans— Philemon)

PETER (Simon) in Matthew 10, 16—17, 26; Mark 3, 8—9, 14; Luke 6, 9, 22; John 13, 18, 21; Acts 1—4, 8, 10—12, 15; Galatians 2; and First and Second Peter

PHILIP the evangelist, in Acts 8

PILATE in Matthew 27, Mark 15, Luke 22—23, and John 18—19

RACHEL in Genesis 29—35

RAHAB in Joshua 2, 6:22-23; and Hebrews 11:31

REBEKAH in Genesis 24—28

REHOBOAM in First Kings 11— 12, 14; First Chronicles 3; Second Chronicles 10—12

RUTH in the book of Ruth

SAMSON in Judges 13—16

SAMUEL in the book of First Samuel

SARAH in Genesis 11—25

SAUL (the king) in First Samuel 9—31

SHADRACH, MESHACH, and ABEDNEGO in Daniel 1, 3

SILAS in Acts 15, 16—18

SOLOMON in Second Samuel 24, First Kings 1—11, First Chronicles 3, and Second Chronicles 1—9

STEPHEN in Acts 6—7

THOMAS in Matthew 1; Mark ; Luke 6; John 11, 14, 20—21; and Acts 1

TIMOTHY in Acts 16—20; First Corinthians 4, 16; and First Timothy 1

UZZIAH in Second Kings 15, First Chronicles 6, and Second Chronicles 26

ZECHARIAH, father of John the Baptist, in Luke 1

ZERUBBABEL in Ezra 2—3, Nehemiah 7, Haggai 1—2, and Zechariah 4

Miracles of Jesus

Signs that Pointed to God!

READ ABOUT HOW JESUS...

Calmed a storm in Matt. 8:23-27, Mark 4:35-41, and Luke 8:22-25

Fed five thousand people in Matt. 14:15-21, Mark 6:35-44, Luke 9:12-17, John 6:5-14

Fed four thousand people in Matt. 15:32-38, Mark 8:1-9

Freed a girl from a demon in Matt. 15:21-28, Mark 7:24-30

Gave life to a widow's dead son in Luke 7:11-16

Gave sight to blind Bartimaeus in Matt. 20:29-34, Mark 10:46-52, Luke 18:35-43

Gave two blind men their sight in Matt. 9:27-31

Healed a bleeding woman in Matt. 9:20-22, Mark 5:25-34, Luke 8:43-48

Healed a blind man in Mark 8:22-26

Healed a boy with an evil spirit in Matt. 17:14-21, Mark 9:14-29, Luke 9:37-42

Healed a crippled woman in Luke 13:10-17

Healed a demon-possessed man who was blind and couldn't talk in Matt. 12:22, Luke 11:14

Healed a lame man in John 5:1-16

Healed a leper in Matt. 8:1-4, Mark 1:40-45, Luke 5:12-15

Healed a man born blind in John 9:1-7

Healed a man by sending demons from his body into a herd of pigs in Matt. 8:28-34, Mark 5:1-20, Luke 8:26-39

Healed a man who couldn't speak in Matt. 9:32-33

Healed a Man who couldn't speak or hear in Mark 7:31-37

Healed a man with dropsy in Luke 14:1-6
Healed a man's ear that had been cut off in Luke 22:49-51
Healed a man's shriveled hand in Matt. 12:9-13,
    Mark 3:1-5, Luke 6:6-11
Healed a soldier's servant in Matt. 8:5-13, Luke 7:1-10
Healed an officer's Son in John 4:46-54
Healed Peter's mother-in-law in Matt. 8:14-17, Mark 1:29-31,
    Luke 4:38-39
Healed ten lepers in Luke 17:11-19
Led the disciples to a miraculous catch of fish in Luke 5:1-11
Led the disciples to a second miraculous catch of fish in John
    21:1-14
Raised Jairus' daughter from the dead in Matt. 9:18-26, Mark
    5:22-43, Luke 8:41-56
Raised Lazarus from the dead in John 11:1-45
Sent an evil spirit out of a man in Mark 1:23-27, Luke 4:33-36
Told Peter to catch a fish with a coin in its mouth in Matt.
    17:24-27
Turned water into wine in John 2:1-11
Walked on water in Matt. 14:22-33, Mark 6:45-52, John 6:17-21

Parables of Jesus

Stories that Make You Think!

READ ABOUT...

THE SEED AND THE SOILS in Matthew 13:3-8, Mark 4:4-8,
Luke 8:5-8

WEEDS in Matthew 13:24-30

A MUSTARD SEED in Matthew 13:31-32, Mark 4:30-32,
Luke 13:18-19

YEAST in Matthew 13:33, Luke 13:20-21

A TREASURE in Matthew 13:44

A PEARL in Matthew 13:45-46

THE FISHING NET in Matthew 13:47-50

THE GROWING GRAIN in Mark 4:26-29

WORKERS IN THE VINEYARD in Matthew 20:1-16

THREE SERVANTS AND THE LOANED MONEY (the "Talents") in
Matthew 25:14-30

AN IMPORTANT MAN'S THREE SERVANTS in Luke 19:11-27

WHAT A SERVANT DESERVES in Luke 17:7-10

A FRIEND AT MIDNIGHT in Luke 11:5-8

A BAD JUDGE in Luke 18:1-8

THE GOOD SAMARITAN in Luke 10:30-37

WHO SITS WHERE AT A WEDDING FEAST in Luke 14:7-11

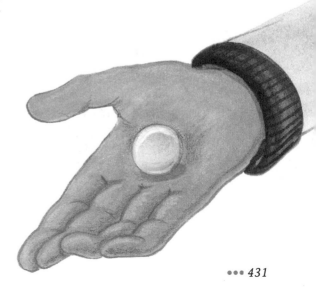

Favorite Read-Aloud Passages

The Creation of the World • *Genesis 1:1—2:3*
Abraham and Isaac • *Genesis 22*
Jacob's Ladder • *Genesis 28:10-22*
Moses and the Burning Bush • *Exodus 2*
The Exodus • *Exodus 12-13*
The Ten Commandments • *Exodus 20*
The Battle of Jericho • *Joshua 6*
Gideon and the "Fleece" • *Judges 6—7*
God Calls the Boy Samuel • *1 Samuel 1—3*
David and Goliath • *1 Samuel 17*
The Lord Is My Shepherd • *Psalm 23*
A Time and Season for Everything • *Ecclesiastes 3:1-8*
Elijah on Mount Carmel • *1 Kings 18*
Elisha's Miracles • *2 Kings 4-5*
Jonah and the Fish • *Jonah 1*
Ezekiel and the Dry Bones • *Ezekiel 37*
Daniel in the Lions' Den • *Daniel 6*
The Birth of Jesus • *Luke 2*
The Baptism of Jesus • *Mark 1:9-11*
The Temptation of Jesus • *Luke 4:1-13*
The "Beatitudes" • *Matthew 5:1-12*
The Lord's Prayer • *Matthew 6:5-15*
The Golden Rule • *Luke 6:31*
Jesus Clears the Temple • *John 2:12-25*
You Must Be Born Again • *John 3:1-21*
Jesus the Living Water • *John 4:4-38*

Bible Reading Calendar

PLAN A: *A Taste of Every Book*

By following the plan below, in 52 weeks (one year)
you'll read a *part* of EVERY BOOK in the Bible.

- [ ] Week 1: Matthew 5, 6, and 7
- [ ] Week 2: *Genesis 1, 2, 3, and 4*
- [ ] Week 3: Matthew 13, 14, and 15
- [ ] Week 4: *Genesis 6, 7, 8, and 9*
- [ ] Week 5: Matthew 26, 27, and 28
- [ ] Week 6: *Genesis 12, 15, 21, and 22*
- [ ] Week 7: Mark 1, 2, 3, and 4
- [ ] Week 8: *Genesis 27, 28, 37, and 39*
- [ ] Week 9: Mark 5, 6, 7, and 8
- [ ] Week 10: *Genesis 41, 42, 43, 44, and 45*
- [ ] Week 11: Mark 9, 10, 11, and 12
- [ ] Week 12: *Exodus 3, 4, 5, and 11*
- [ ] Week 13: Mark 13, 14, 15, and 16
- [ ] Week 14: *Exodus 12, 13, 14, and 15*
- [ ] Week 15: Luke 1, 2, 10, and 15
- [ ] Week 16: *Leviticus 26; Deuteronomy 4, 8, and 28*

- ☐ Week 17: Luke 16, 22, 23, and 24
- ☐ Week 18: *Joshua 2, 6, 7, and 24*
- ☐ Week 19: John 3, 6, 9, and 10
- ☐ Week 20: *Judges 2, 6, and 7; and Ruth 1*
- ☐ Week 21: John 13, 14, 15, and 16
- ☐ Week 22: *1 Samuel 3, 16, 17, and 20*
- ☐ Week 23: John 17, 18, 19, and 21
- ☐ Week 24: *2 Samuel 6, 7, 11, and 12*
- ☐ Week 25: Acts 1, 2, 5, and 9
- ☐ Week 26: *1 Kings 3, 9, 17, and 18*
- ☐ Week 27: Acts 16, 17, 26, 27, and 28
- ☐ Week 28: *2 Kings 2, 4, 17, and 22*
- ☐ Week 29: Romans 3, 4, 5, and 6
- ☐ Week 30: *1 Chronicles 11; 2 Chronicles 10, 11, and 26*
- ☐ Week 31: Romans 8, 12, 13, and 14
- ☐ Week 32: *Ezra 3; Nehemiah 4, and Esther 4*
- ☐ Week 33: 1 Corinthians 1, 3, and 13
- ☐ Week 34: *Job 1, 2, 38, and 42*
- ☐ Week 35: 2 Corinthians 4, 5, and 6
- ☐ Week 36: *Psalm 16 and 145; Proverbs 3 and 22*

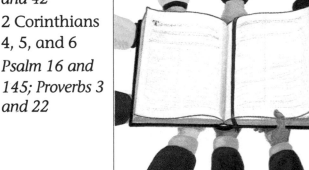

PLAN B: *The Entire Bible*

By following the plan below, in 52 weeks (one year)
you'll read ALL of every book in the Bible.

☐   Week 1:   Genesis 1—35

☐   Week 2:   *Matthew 1—10*

☐   Week 3:   Genesis 35—50; and Exodus 1—20

☐   Week 4:   *Matthew 11—20*

☐   Week 5:   Exodus 21—40; and Leviticus 1—15

☐   Week 6:   *Matthew 21—28; and Mark 1—2*

☐   Week 7:   Leviticus 16—27; and Numbers 1—13

☐   Week 8:   *Mark 3—12*

☐   Week 9:   Numbers 14—36; and Deuteronomy 1—12

☐   Week 10:   *Mark 13—16; and Luke 1—6*

☐   Week 11:   Deuteronomy 13—34; and Joshua 1—13

☐   Week 12:   *Luke 7—16*

☐   Week 13:   Joshua 14—24; and Judges 1—14

☐   Week 14:   *Luke 17—24; and John 1—2*

☐   Week 15:   Judges 15—21; all of Ruth; and 1 Samuel 1—24

☐   Week 16:   *John 3—12*

☐   Week 17:   1 Samuel 25—31; all of 2 Samuel; and 1 Kings 1—4

☐ Week 18: *John 13—21; and Acts 1*

☐ Week 19: 1 Kings 5—22; and 2 Kings 1—17

☐ Week 20: *Acts 2—11*

☐ Week 21: 2 Kings 18—25; and 1 Chronicles 1—27

☐ Week 22: *Acts 12—21*

☐ Week 23: 1 Chronicles 28—29; and 2 Chronicles 1—33

☐ Week 24: *Acts 22—28; and Romans 1—3*

☐ Week 25: 2 Chronicles 34—36; and all of Ezra, Nehemiah, and Esther

☐ Week 26: *Romans 4—13*

☐ Week 27: Job 1—35

☐ Week 28: *Romans 14—16; and 1 Corinthians 1—7*

☐ Week 29: Job 36—42; and Psalms 1—28

☐ Week 30: *1 Corinthians 8—16; and 2 Corinthians 1*

☐ Week 31: Psalms 29—63

☐ Week 32: *2 Corinthians 2—11*

☐ Week 33: Psalm 64—98

☐ Week 34: *2 Corinthians 12—13; all of Galatians; and Ephesians 1—2*

☐ Week 35: Psalm 99—133

☐ Week 36: *Ephesians 3—6; all of Philippians; and Colossians 1—2*

☐ Week 37: Psalm 134—150; and Proverbs 1—18

☐ Week 38: *Colossians 3—4; all of 1 Thessalonians and 2 Thessalonians*

☐ Week 39: Proverbs 19—31; all of Ecclesiastes and Song of Solomon; and Isaiah 1—3

☐ Week 40: *All of 1 Timothy and 2 Timothy*

☐ Week 41: Isaiah 4—38

☐ Week 42: *All of Titus and Philemon; and Hebrews 1—6*

☐ Week 43: Isaiah 39—66; and Jeremiah 1—7

☐ Week 44: *Hebrews 7—13; and James 1—3*

☐ Week 45: Jeremiah 8—42

☐ Week 46: *James 4—5; and all of 1 Peter and 2 Peter*

☐ Week 47: Jeremiah 43—52; all of Lamentations; and Ezekiel 1—22

☐ Week 48: *All of 1 John, 2 John, 3 John, and Jude; and Revelation 1—2*

☐ Week 49: Ezekiel 23—48; and all of Daniel

☐ Week 50: *Revelation 3—12*

☐ Week 51: All of Hosea, Joel, Amos, Obadiah, Jonah, Micah, Nahum, Habakkuk, Zephaniah, Haggai, Zechariah, and Malachi

☐ Week 52: *Revelation 13—22*

PLAN C: *Big-Picture Reading!*

By following the plan below, in 52 weeks (one year),
you'll read all of the New Testament twice and the
Old Testament once. And you'll do it without splitting up
any of the books (except Psalms), giving you a better
"big-picture" view of all the Bible.

☐ Week 1: Genesis

☐ Week 2: *Matthew*

☐ Week 3: Exodus

☐ Week 4: *Mark*

☐ Week 5: Leviticus

☐ Week 6: *Luke*

☐ Week 7: Numbers

☐ Week 8: *John*

☐ Week 9: Deuteronomy

☐ Week 10: *Acts*

☐ Week 11: Joshua, Judges

☐ Week 12: *Romans*

☐ Week 13: Ruth, 1 Samuel

☐ Week 14: *1 and 2 Corinthians*

☐ Week 15: 2 Samuel

☐ Week 16: *Galatians, Ephesians, Philippians*

☐ Week 17: 1 Kings

☐ Week 18: *Colossians, 1 and 2 Thessalonians, 1 and 2 Timothy*

☐ Week 19: 2 Kings

☐ Week 20: *Titus, Philemon, Hebrews*

☐ Week 21: 1 Chronicles

☐ Week 22: *James, 1 and 2 Peter*

☐ Week 23: 2 Chronicles

☐ Week 24: *1, 2, and 3 John, Jude*

☐ Week 25: Ezra, Nehemiah, Esther

☐ Week 26: *Revelation*

☐ Week 27: Job

Scripture Index

Teaching Guide

A PLAN FOR USING
THE BIBLE TELLS ME SO
IN WEEKLY CLASSES...

WEEK 1: Read and discuss Chapters 1 and 2; the *Question Corner* on page 44; and the *Discovery* on page 45.

WEEK 2: Read and discuss Chapters 3 and 4; the *Question Corner* on page 76; and the *Discovery* on page 77.

WEEK 3: Read and discuss Chapters 5 and 6; the *Question Corner* on page 102; and the *Discovery* on page 103.

WEEK 4: Read and discuss Chapters 7 and 8; the *Question Corner* on page 122; and the *Discovery* on page 123.

WEEK 5: Read and discuss Chapters 9 and 10; the *Question Corner* on page 148; and the *Discovery* on page 149.

WEEK 6: Read and discuss Chapters 11 and 12; the *Question Corner* on page 170; and the *Discovery* on page 171.

WEEK 7:   Read and discuss Chapter 13; the
            Question Corner on page 192; and the
            Discovery on page 193.

WEEK 8:   Read and discuss Chapters 14 and 15; the
            Question Corner on page 220; and the
            Discovery on page 221.

WEEK 9:   Read and discuss Chapters 16 and 17; the
            Question Corner on page 244; and the
            Discovery on page 245.

WEEK 10:   Read and discuss Chapters 18 and 19; the
            Question Corner on page 266; and the
            Discovery on page 267.

WEEK 11:   Read and discuss Chapters 20 and 21; the
            Question Corner on page 306; and the
            Discovery on page 307.

WEEK 12:   Read and discuss Chapters 22 and 23; and
            the *Question Corner* on page 348.

WEEK 13:   Explore the "Taking a Look, Book by Book"
            section beginning on page 350, as well as
            the "More Discoveries" section beginning on
            page 406. Also, look over the *Bible Reading
            Calendar* (pages and explore possibilities for
            commitments to a Bible reading program.

Each week, you may also want to consider exploring a few
pages in "Taking a Look, Book by Book" (beginning on
page 350), and in "More Discoveries" (page 406).

Gold 'n' Honey
BOOKS